MARTIN LUTHER'S NINETY-FIVE THESES

MARTIN LUTHER'S
95 THESES

WITH THE PERTINENT DOCUMENTS
FROM THE HISTORY OF THE REFORMATION

Edited by Kurt Aland

CONCORDIA PUBLISHING HOUSE · SAINT LOUIS

CONTENTS

PREFACE TO THE ENGLISH EDITION

The Foundation for Reformation Research has stated as one of its objectives: to stimulate historical research concerning the Protestant Reformation and to publish the results of such historical research. The foundation did not actually stimulate the research for this volume, but it recognized its value and encouraged the translation into English.

Kurt Aland's work on the Ninety-five Theses came to the attention of A. O. Fuerbringer, acting executive director of the foundation at the time, in the summer of 1966. Agreements were soon made to have the foundation support a translation with the approval of Furche-Verlag, the German publisher. Upon his return from Europe, Dr. Fuerbringer turned the work over to three persons: J. A. Hinz, who reviewed the book and noted those parts that had already been translated; P. J. Schroeder, who did a trial translation of the introduction; and P. D. Pahl, who translated most of the previously untranslated texts. The American Edition of Luther's Works was used wherever possible, and the foundation expresses its appreciation to the publishers, Concordia Publishing House and Fortress Press [now Augsburg Fortress], for permission to use these translations. The translators of the American Edition portions of the texts are: H. J. Grimm, E. W. Gritsch, C. M. Jacobs, G. G. Krodel, L. W. Spitz Sr., and L. W. Spitz Jr. Their contributions are identified in the table of contents. The editing was done by the staff of the foundation and of Concordia Publishing House.

The Inter-Lutheran Consultation [that is, the committee of The Lutheran Church—Missouri Synod] for the celebration for the 450th Reformation anniversary (LIFE—NEW LIFE) has made this effort possible with a grant to the foundation and through the foundation to Concordia Publishing House.

This "workbook," as Aland calls his book, is intended to be a scholarly, readable treatment of a difficult historical problem; but it can also serve as a model for other studies of similar problems. His efforts lay the groundwork for a penetrating evaluation of the question: Why do we celebrate 31 October 1517? And so we are back where we started: to stimulate historical research . . .

The Foundation for Reformation Research
R. E. Diener, Executive Director
St. Louis, Missouri, 1967

Abbreviations

CR   Bretschneider, C. D., and H. E. Bindseil, eds. *Corpus Reformatorum*. Halle: Schwetschke, 1834–1860.

LW   Luther, Martin. *Luther's Works*. American Edition. General editors Jaroslav Pelikan and Helmut T. Lehmann. St. Louis: Concordia, and Philadelphia: Muhlenberg and Fortress, 1955–1986.

MPL   Migne, J. P., ed. *Patrologia, Series Latina*. 221 vols. Paris: n.p., 1884–1904.

WA   Luther, Martin. *D. Martin Luthers Werke. Kritische Gesamtausgabe. Schriften.* 68 vols. Wiemar: Hermann Böhlaus Nachfolger, 1883–1999.

WABr   Luther, Martin. *D. Martin Luthers Werke. Kritische Gesamtausgabe. Briefwechsel.* Wiemar: Hermann Böhlaus Nachfolger, 1930–1985.

WATr   Luther, Martin. *D. Martin Luthers Werke. Kritische Gesamtausgabe. Tischreden.* Wiemar: Hermann Böhlaus Nachfolger, 1912–1921. Reprinted in 2000.

Introduction

Even before 31 October 1517, Martin Luther was one of the leading professors at the University of Wittenberg. To reach this position took some time and cost not a few conflicts. He had been a member of the faculty already in 1508/1509, and after an absence he returned in the summer of 1511 for permanent service. Promoted to doctor of theology in October 1512, he ultimately took over the chair of biblical studies of the theological faculty as successor to the influential and renowned John Staupitz. At that time Luther was the youngest member of the theological faculty, a group that still retained the prescribed patterns of medieval theology.[1] And his efforts to move this faculty away from Scholastic theology into the direction of St. Augustine and St. Paul met with no success at first. Not until 1515 did the situation improve. By then his lectures had not only attracted a considerable audience but were already becoming so favorably known that many a student transferred to the University of Wittenberg solely because of Professor Luther's fame. The Augustinian Eremite order appointed him district vicar, that is, superior and supervisor over the six monasteries in central Germany. Among the people at the court of his prince, Elector Frederick the Wise, Luther found a true friend and convinced follower in the court preacher and secretary, George Spalatin. But the faculty and the university still opposed any innovation.

To promote progress, Luther had his students (at the time still comparatively few in number) present at graduations such theses as would call forth discussion about any innovation. We know that as late as September 1516 such a series of theses (defended by Bartholomew Bern-hardi of Feldkirch) brought about violent opposition by the professors of theology at Wittenberg. Any number of private discussions may have preceded this public clash, but this was the first to lead to decisions. A few professors were finally convinced that the shocking opinions of Luther actually corresponded, in word or thought, to those of the church father St. Augustine—and after all, St. Augustine was the patron of the whole university!

As a direct result of the disputation of 1516, Andreas Carlstadt, pro-fessor at the university since its founding and the one who, as dean of the faculty at the time, had received Luther's doctoral oath and had placed the doctor's biretta on his head, went to Leipzig in January 1517 to pur-chase an edition of the works of St. Augustine. Up to that time he neither owned a copy nor studied St. Augustine to any extent. Now when he had thoroughly immersed himself in St. Augustine's writings, he recog-nized that Luther was correct in supporting his statements by references to St. Augustine. Once he was won over to St. Augustine, Carlstadt informed the university of this conversion. In no fewer than 151 theses, he defended his new insights on 26 April. Thus Luther prevailed within the faculty. In his joy, Luther could write to his friend John Lang at Erfurt on 18 May 1517: "Our theology and St. Augustine are making rapid headway with God's help and are becoming determinative at the university."[2] Only he who lectures on Scripture, St. Augustine, or some other church father, Luther continued, can depend on an audience; medieval Scholastic theology no longer holds any attraction.

What did this victory of Luther at the University of Wittenberg in the spring of 1517 mean for the public, either the learned ranks or the ecclesiastical community? Very little, practically nothing! We dare not forget: This university was a mere fifteen years old at the time. Even if we omit the famous schools abroad, such as Paris, Bologna, Oxford, and Cambridge, there were at least fourteen universities in Germany at that time, and many of them had been in existence for a century and longer. When Frederick the Wise established the University of Wittenberg in 1502, there were only twenty-two professional chairs. Of these, fifteen had to be supplied by the clergy of All Saints' Church and the Wittenberg cloisters, so the university had only seven chairs that were not estab-lished by the church. Even in 1532, Luther used to think that in Wittenberg a person stood "at the border of civilization."[3] When he came to Wittenberg, he was surprised that anyone would establish a university there.[4] As late as 1539, Luther stated that even though the electors had done much for Wittenberg, it had not yet become a city.[5] These assertions of Luther certainly appear to be exaggerations, but he was not alone in his evaluation. Friends and foes of the Reformation made similar statements. So we ought not conceive of too grandiose a picture of Wittenberg at the beginning of the sixteenth century. At the time, Wittenberg lay at the very edge of the civilized world. What happened there was of little concern to men of learning and of the church. This situation definitely still prevailed in September 1517. Professor Luther had seen to the posting of ninety-seven theses, which his pupil, Franz Günther from Nordhausen, was to debate on 4 September 1517. They were directed "against Scholastic theology" and summarized programmatically, sharply, and critically what Luther had to say. It is known that Luther sent the theses at least to Erfurt and Nuremberg with the request that they be given wider dissemination. And this was done—but the anticipated reaction did not materialize. No doubt Luther did find out that the people at his alma mater were angry with him and that his teachers charged him with presumptuousness. But they remained silent and, contrary to his hope and desire, did not enter into a learned discussion with him. Even Professor Eck of Ingolstadt remained silent, though the theses were also sent to him at Luther's instigation. The ninety-seven theses with which Luther had hoped to initiate a reform of the traditional methodology of scholarship and of the study of theology remained a shot in the dark.

So Luther was one of the leading professors at the University of Wittenberg by 31 October 1517. He had begun to be respected and influential even outside the Wittenberg area. Unfortunately, however, his voice was heard by only a few. In the constellations of learned men, he was still a star of lowest magnitude. The church took no notice of him at all. All of that changed on 31 October 1517 with one blow. To be precise, we might say with a few hammer blows, namely, with those with which he nailed the Ninety-five Theses to the door of the Castle Church in Wittenberg. From a merely locally respected but otherwise relatively unknown and unnoticed professor in Wittenberg, Luther became in an amazingly short time a personality known within Germany and beyond its border, loved and praised but at the same time also feared and maligned, in contemporary church circles as well as in intellectual circles generally. Within fourteen days, Luther said, his theses had traversed all of Germany.[6] Formerly this statement was held to be an exaggeration. But we have a report of a discussion Caesar Pflug, counselor of Duke George of Saxony, had with Bishop Adolf of Merseburg before 27 November 1517: "It is gratifying also to His Grace (Bishop Adolf) that the poor people who were running around and searching for indulgence have been warned of the chicanery of Tetzel and that the *Conclusiones* (the Ninety-five Theses) by the Augustinian monk of Wittenberg have been posted at many places; that will cause a great disruption for indulgences."[7] Obviously the Ninety-five Theses were known to all who were involved, at least by name and basic content, for Pflug did not deem it necessary to present any commentary to his prince. And around the same time or shortly thereafter the theses were also known in Hamburg. For we know that Albert Krantz, one of the leading citizens of Hamburg, read a copy of the Ninety-five Theses on his deathbed (he died on 7 December 1517) and discussed them with his friends.[8] In Nuremberg there was a copy of the Ninety-five Theses apparently almost immediately after their posting because a printed version of the theses, as well as a German translation, were in preparation already in November 1517—unless all appearances are deceiving.[9] At any rate, the Ninety-five Theses were known at the court at Lochau (near Torgau), as well as at Wittenberg itself immediately after 31 October. From a letter of Luther to Spalatin in the early part of November (p. 71), we learn that at the time Spalatin had already inquired of Luther about the theses and that at Wittenberg the idea prevailed among many that the elector had something to do with them. This presupposes a widespread knowledge of the theses at Lochau. What Caesar Pflug reported probably applied not to an already accomplished fact but to a plan of Duke George, who got the consent of Bishop Adolf (or was it the bishop's own plan?), to have the theses posted in many places in a German translation (only thus could they be of help to the simple people about whom they were speaking). But finally it is unquestionable that the theses were known in Merseburg as well as in Dresden. And if they are to be found simultaneously or shortly after also in Hamburg and probably previously in Nuremberg (in all cases without Luther's sending them there himself), we must assume their appearance in an amazingly short period of time throughout all Germany. Even at the end of his life, Luther told of a letter he had received from his friend John Fleck, prior of the Franciscan monastery Stein-Lausitz near Bitterfeld, immediately after he had heard about the theses. He wrote Luther words of encouragement for his project and inspired him to go on. To his monks the prior said, "He is here who will do the task."[10]

"He is here who will do the task." How the Ninety-five Theses were received the example of Albrecht Dürer indicates. Immediately after he had read the theses (obviously in a German translation), he sent Luther a few of his copperplates and woodcuts. Developments proceeded at a swift pace. Bishop Albert of Mainz got to see the Ninety-five Theses near the end of November and immediately lodged a protest against Luther in Rome (Luther's letter of 31 October to the bishop containing the theses was finally opened at Calbe on 17 November and was forwarded to Aschaffenburg, the bishop's residence at the time). In January 1518, the German Dominicans met in assembly at Frankfort on the Oder, and Tetzel defended his 106 theses directed against Luther. At the same time the decision was made to lodge the second complaint against Luther in Rome. Eck now began his attack against Luther in a literary work, but one that was distributed only in handwritten form. That initiated a pamphlet battle that eventually led to the disputation at Leipzig in July 1519. Carlstadt published theses against Eck; Eck answered him with other theses. Because these were directed for all practical purposes against Luther, he also published thirteen theses. The Augustinian order protected Luther and gave him time to articulate his position in a disputation at a conference of the order in Heidelberg. But stronger and more numerous voices were being raised to call Luther a heretic and to predict his imminent death at the stake. The appearance of a sharp tirade against Luther by Silvester Prierias, the inquisitor of the Roman Curia and one of its most influential men, seemed to guarantee the doom of Luther.[11] Of course, the processes against him in the Curia were already in full swing. It resulted in the summons of Luther to Rome to account for the charges raised against him. The citation reached Luther on 7 August 1518. That is directly attributable to the special political situation of those months. The succession of Emperor Maximilian was to be settled, and Luther's prince, Elector Frederick the Wise, had a key position in the deliberations. The wish of the elector to have Luther tried in Germany was granted. But the cardinal did not succeed in maneuvering Luther into a retraction. Instead, both men opposed each other vehemently. Despite all that, the opposition proceeded against Luther only with some hesitance, for the solution to the succession problem was becoming more and more critical. When Emperor Maximilian died in January 1519, the Curia actually went so far as to request that Frederick the Wise be named his successor. The Curia wanted to prevent the rule of Germany and of the worldwide Spanish kingdom to come under one head, as actually happened with Charles V. Under these conditions, an energetic attack against Luther was out of the question, for his prince held a protective hand over him. On the contrary, some were apparently ready to make Luther a cardinal should Frederick want it. Only when Charles (indeed, with the support of Frederick) received the imperial dignity at the end of June 1519 was the need for caution removed. Immediately the demand was renewed to apprehend Luther. But when this did not meet with success, a bull was drawn up threatening him with excommunication.

The bull was printed in complete form in June 1520, sent to Germany, and distributed in the fall. On 10 December 1520 Luther burned the bull at the Elster Gate in Wittenberg. This happened after papal representatives in many places had already committed Luther's writings to the faggots with due ceremony. The significance we attach to Luther's act today is far different from what his contemporaries thought. To them the really provocative act on 10 December 1520 was Luther's burning of the books of canon law together with the writings of the Scholastic theologians and his Roman opponents. The burning of canon law—the basic document not only of the Roman Church of that day but also of great significance to secular governments in many areas—was a revolutionary act. It shocked even the close friends of Luther. From now on there would be no turning back. That the excommunication threatened in the first bull finally became an actuality was hardly a surprise. It was for some time no longer necessary to affirm explicitly that Luther had been outlawed by the church. The Imperial Diet of Worms in the spring of 1521 attached the ban of emperor and empire to the condemnation of the church.

All of these incidents had their preludes and postludes. From 31 October 1517 right up to Luther's enforced isolation at the Wartburg, which came as a result of the Diet of Worms, his life was filled with tensions and irritating altercations and decision making. In addition to these demands, which are really sufficient in themselves to exhaust the strength of one man, there were commitments at Wittenberg, the continuing teaching and preaching programs. But what had been initiated within the narrow confines of Wittenberg had gained an altogether different range and power since 31 October 1517. Students were streaming into Wittenberg from all areas, hundreds of them sitting at Luther's feet. Nor was this drawing power confined to students. Even accomplished scholars who had already completed their own academic work wanted to come to the university to hear Luther or Melanchthon, who since August 1518 had done much to lead the Wittenberg theological faculty and university out of their former isolation and to guarantee that the most careful attention in the church and the learned community of Germany and Europe would be focused on whatever happened to them. Before the appearance of the Ninety-five Theses, Luther had published several other series of theses. In 1516, he had published an edition of the *German Theology* with a brief introductory word. In 1517, he had written an exposition on the seven penitential psalms. But that was the extent of his published works up to the time of the posting of the Ninety-five Theses. Actually the series of theses should not be listed with his other works up to that time because they were designed for the limited intellectual community and certainly not for the general public. They were written for a comparatively small circle of professional theologians.

The year 1518 brought a decided change. One has to look at a chronological list of Luther's works to see that it is not enough to designate the year 1518 as the beginning of his public career. Rather, one must speak of a veritable explosion that had its inception here and now continued through the years. It soon became apparent that a single publisher was in no position to set and print Luther's writings. He kept numerous printers busy and yet complained that his manuscripts were piling up because the printers were unable to keep up. Luther's writings at first dealt directly with the Ninety-five Theses. In German he published his "A Sermon on Indulgence and Grace" and explained once again the basic thought contained in the theses, but in simple and easily understood language for the general public. Then followed the Latin *Resolutions*, in which each one of the Ninety-five Theses is exhaustively explained and documented. He defended his "Sermon" against the attack of Tetzel. Each one of these writings called forth an exceptional response—so great, in fact, that the "Sermon" went through fourteen editions in 1518 and twelve more editions appeared up to the year 1520. Of the defense of the "Sermon," we have eighteen different editions.

Soon, however, Luther's writings went beyond the area of indulgences. Already in 1518 the pamphlet battle about the theses included a discussion of the problem of excommunication by the church together with the related problem of the relation of the pope to the church and of his plenipotentiary powers. In 1519, Luther added his discussion of the primacy of the pope and of the possibility that councils may err. In 1520, he wrote on the church's invalid claim that there were seven sacraments, on the matter of the reform of the church in head and members, and on a new morality—in short, on the whole range of the new faith. Yet there were unresolved problems: monasticism, the Mass, and others. Not only will any student of Luther's writings and sermons after 1517 be clearly and obviously impressed with the number and effectiveness of his writings, he also will be sensitive to the extremely wide range of his works (of the sermons and the practical and edificatory expositions of Scripture, as well as of the scholarly works) and note how these continued to multiply with persistent regularity and with an almost explosive force.

In his reflections on the Reformation, Luther always placed its beginnings in the time of the indulgence controversy.[12] He never specifically referred to the Ninety-five Theses but only mentioned that in 1517 he had begun to write against indulgences, or against the pope.[13] And one time ten years later, when he was recollecting the events of 1517 in a sort of anniversary memorial,[14] he did not speak of the Ninety-five Theses but of "the tenth year since the elimination of indulgences."[15] The Ninety-five Theses were just a spark; much more important was the chain reaction activated by them. If Luther had had just an inkling of the effect the theses were to have, he would have structured them differently, he said in 1518.[16] It was the tremendous reactionary effect against the Ninety-five Theses and the attack they loosed against his person that motivated Luther to a thorough rethinking and documentation of the indulgence issue. At the time, 31 October 1517, indulgences were not yet strictly defined by the church, so it was thought to be permissible to debate freely on the subject. Luther could even think that his viewpoint would merit the thanks and recognition of the authorities in the church.[17] In this he was deceived. The instructions given to the indulgence preachers were not distortions, as Luther had assumed, but represented official church teaching, a teaching that was then promptly and ceremoniously proclaimed in 1518. But behind it all—and this was the worst of it for Luther—there was a concept of the church, of the status of the pope, of justification, of the Christian faith in general that Luther felt he must oppose with all the power and zeal he possessed. This became clear to him in piecemeal fashion. It was only with reluctance that he yielded to it, so later on he had a completely negative attitude toward his earlier writings. In them, he says, he did not see the issues clearly enough and was far, far too conciliatory to the pope.[18] Despite his negative appraisal of earlier writings, when he did include them—or better, let them be included—in the complete collection of his earlier works, they were to serve as warning examples.[19] Luther himself was a determined opponent of the collecting of his writings, for he wanted to let them perish in favor of exclusive Bible reading.

Thus the Reformation began with the Ninety-five Theses. Of that there can be no doubt. But if at Luther's time anyone thought at all about beginnings—there was actually too much to do in the way of realizing and maintaining the movement to allow time for anniversary celebrations—if such a function was at all contemplated, the prime consideration was the place or locale in memory of the day of the first evangelical preaching or the day of the official introduction of the Reformation. Or else the anniversary of the Augsburg Confession was commemorated as the first official formulation of the new faith. In any case 31 October was not generally thought of at all for the first. The posting of theses at that time was nothing unusual but rather a routine matter. In the academic community disputations were a prescribed part of the course, and for acquiring an academic degree they were even mandatory. Every disputation called for the presentation of theses to be posted according to specific regulations. In Wittenberg it was customary to post theses on church doors. Because the Castle Church was also the university church, its doors served as the "bulletin board" of the university. Whenever a professor desired to speak on a topic of current interest or wished to reveal new results of his work, he could use the graduation or the doctoral type of disputation (the theses were always composed by the professor and not by the one to be advanced to a degree). Or else he could call for a special disputation, as Luther did with the Ninety-five Theses. In this case no date was set as in the other types. The opponents had to be called to battle first, accept the challenge, and prepare for the debate before it could take place. In normal disputations the opponents stood ready beforehand, and they were often taking part in a mere sham battle or a good show. This was a summons to a real contest. In a university town it often happened that the actual contest caused much more of a sensation than did the challenge. In the case of the Ninety-five Theses nothing happened; there was no one in Wittenberg who wanted to oppose Luther in debate. Tetzel selected the University of Frankfort on the Oder and the background of a private meeting of the Dominican order to defend his theses against Luther. Eck's wrath spent itself in annotations that never reached public print. If one of them or even a less prominent theologian had appeared for an actual debate on the Ninety-five Theses against Luther, Wittenberg and environs would have been a lively scene. Many visitors would have come to the city, and official records would have been written, and on and on. And we would know many significant details about the event. When Luther—possibly about noon of 31 October 1517—posted the theses on the door of the Castle Church, he did so on his own and did not have it done by the university proctor, as was the regulation according to the rules of disputations. In modern terms, Luther posted a notice about twice the size of a piece of typing paper on the bulletin board of the university.

This rather commonplace act got little or no attention from anyone. If someone did stop to read the theses, his first impulse was either to write down the contents or to attempt to get a printed copy, if that were available. Those who received a copy from Luther[20] passed it on to someone else. Printers and publishers from out of town got hold of this very popular item and reprinted the theses for rapid sale. Translations were prepared and disseminated in print.[21] Thus the Ninety-five Theses began their victory march through Germany. Their explosive force lay in the subject matter and in the manner in which this was treated. What was of interest was their content, not the manner in which they were first made public. Two years later people seldom thought of them, for in the meantime the controversy had arrived at an entirely different stage. The Ninety-five Theses had been long outdated. Soon people thought of them only as they began to reflect on their significance—and that meant, under normal conditions, not at all for the first. Only after Luther's death in 1546 do the first approaches to such reflection appear. By that time the first epoch of the Reformation—we might call it the heroic period—had passed. We tend to look at the first epoch as an accomplished deed, much as we tend to look upon the Lutheran Church as a finished product. In the 1550s, Melanchthon occasionally, but by no means always, mentioned the posting of the theses in the dating of letters he wrote on 31 October. In the biography of Luther written directly after the reformer's death and designed for the second volume of the so-called Wittenberg Edition, Melanchthon recalled the date and place of the posting.[22] Melanchthon was a historian and a scholarly man. Already during Luther's lifetime he often had Luther relate that part of the story of his life and of the Reformation that Melanchthon had not personally experienced.[23] For information on Luther's birthday and youth, for instance, Melanchthon went to Luther's mother.[24] That was necessary because Luther himself was not absolutely sure of the year of his birth. When Melanchthon cited 31 October as the day and named Castle Church as the location of the posting of the theses in the eulogy of his friend, we can depend on the fact of the matter. He wrote less than thirty years after the posting and in the very place where it happened. Enough eyewitnesses of the actual events of the first year of the Reformation were still alive. Had there been any discrepancy in Melanchthon's report, especially the professors and students at Wittenberg would no doubt have called attention to it. Besides, when Melanchthon arrived in Wittenberg in 1518, the Ninety-five Theses were still much a part of conversation. He makes references to this fact in a letter written in 1519[25] and in a writing of 1521.[26]

Although these are casual references, they are still significant because we always have to be aware of how few of those earlier sources have been preserved for us. Just one example will give some indication. On 26 October 1516 Luther wrote: "I need about two copyists or secretaries; all day long I do almost nothing but write letters."[27] Yet out of all that correspondence of the year 1516 there are extant only twenty-one letters of Luther. On 31 October 1517 the correspondence of Luther in the Weimar Edition reaches only No. 48. That number represents as many letters as are extant for almost thirty-five years of Luther's life. Up to 31 October

1518 the total goes up to No. 105. For that single year, then, there are more letters extant than for the entire previous period. Up to 31 October 1519 a further 109 letters are added—again more letters preserved for a single year than in the entire previous period. Obviously, Luther wrote more letters every year than previously. But the significant annual increase stems also from the fact that he became better known and more respected from day to day and that the recipients for that reason preserved his letters in increasing numbers. Here, too, 31 October 1517 is a turning point. Whatever took place previous to that date belongs to the "prehistoric period" of the Reformation. Even the months following the posting of the theses and perhaps up to 1520 are to be so reckoned. On 31 October 1517 no one—least of all Luther himself—could have envisioned the significance of the dissemination of the theses nor of their impact on world history. And as the response provoked by the theses extended to ever-widening circles, as Luther was compelled to write one polemical treatise after another against an increasing number of opponents, as questions and problems multiplied and new theological and ecclesiastical issues gradually put indulgences into the background, even then people discovered the real significance of the event only very gradually.

No one at the time even remotely thought of documentation in the modern sense—the establishment of the events by sources and records—for posterity or even only for contemporaries. Besides, people had no time for such pursuits because of the fast pace at which events and tasks tumbled over one another. Probably the only contemporary who had at least a sense for the historical importance—a learned, organized interest—of the events that also shaped his own life was Melanchthon. He was a historian by profession and vocation. And today when critics occasionally complain that there are so few records of the beginnings of the Reformation and that what we have are often unclear and contradictory reports—in this case the situation surrounding the posting of the theses—it should be noted that these critics are thinking in terms of contemporary historiography. The criticism is, to be sure, historically valid and yet unhistorical because they look for a completeness of archival material for a time 450 years ago to match the record taken for granted as available for any modern event of moderate significance. Only where a multiplicity of documents may be taken for granted can incomplete documentation be used as argumentation against the historicity of an event. In earlier centuries the situation was entirely different. Speaking pointedly and even paradoxically, we might say that where a fully detailed set of evidence is extant for the beginnings of a great intellectual movement, we have to be almost suspicious. In the normal course of events—at least in the past and to a certain extent also in the present—the documents show that the responsible agents conducted their affairs without an awareness of what they were actually accomplishing and above all without a view toward future generations. Any deviation from such normal patterns as a rule justifies doubting the real importance of a movement or of its originator. All great intellectual movements of the past have their "prehistoric periods," that is, an early phase in which for reasons already noted not all of the events are so clearly or visibly recorded as we might wish but remain behind a mist that is penetrated only with maximum effort.

At any rate, the day of the posting of the theses was celebrated as the official Reformation Day for the first time on 31 October 1617, its centennial. The second time was the observance in 1667, the sesquicentennial. From that time on celebrations increased in number and became a rather regular institution in which the remembrance of the Reformation became crystallized quite generally on the congregational level. This is both right and wrong: right, in that the storm signal for the Reformation was given with the Ninety-five Theses; wrong, in that the theses and their author were far from intent on initiating such a movement. For a long time Luther still considered himself a faithful adherent of the pope and the Roman Church. It is also wrong in that it is not the posting of the theses but exclusively their content that was effective, as was shown above. Very likely the first direct copies of the theses posted on the door of the Castle Church had significance only in the earliest period. Not until the printers took them over did they enjoy the very wide dissemination with which we are familiar. The content of the theses together with the viewpoint they represented not simply concerning indulgences but concerning justification and the total life and faith of the Christian gave to them their effectiveness. The movement depended on the content of the theses. If the posting of the theses as an event has become very significant for evangelical Christianity, it can only be because of the symbolic value unwittingly ascribed to the act. The significance otherwise attributed to this event does as little justice to what actually happened on 31 October 1517 as the conceptions of those who deny the posting of the theses; it can be explained only as caused by insufficient acquaintance with the history and the conditions of that time.

This introduction, as well as this entire book, grew out of an awareness of these imbalances. In both the introduction and the text, the effort is made to create the conditions for such an acquaintance, for making the reader and that time contemporaneous so far as that can be achieved. In the first part, retrospective views of the whole course of events are brought together: Luther's famous preface from the first volume of the Latin series of the complete Wittenberg Edition of his writings, containing a presentation and an evaluation of his beginnings (pp. 31ff.); then a brief excerpt from his tract "Against Hanswurst" of 1541 (pp. 40ff.), which treats not only the course of events but also their significance; finally, the first part of Melanchthon's preface of 1546 (pp. 44ff.).

In the second part, we present the Ninety-five Theses themselves (pp. 55ff.) and then "A Sermon on Indulgence and Grace" (pp. 63ff.). Both are closely associated and deal with the same subject: the theses for the intellectuals and the sermon for the church. The third part contains in chronological order those letters that pertain to our theme. At the beginning is the letter to Albert Mainz of 31 October 1517 (pp. 69ff.) with which Luther included a copy of the theses. The theses were inserted rather casually, probably after their posting. A careful and unprejudiced reading of this letter will not allow the conclusion reached in one published work on the theses, mainly, that Luther did not post the theses but sent them only to Albert and the Brandenburg bishop as the responsible ecclesiastical authorities.[28] A presentation copy of the Ninety-five Theses to ecclesiastical authority would look entirely different and would not name the subject matter to which the letter is addressed after the day, that is, at the conclusion of the letter in a post-script. Luther's purpose in writing is to persuade the archbishop to rescind the directives given to the indulgence preachers and to change the practice of selling indulgences. Only in concluding the letter does Luther direct him to the theses as evidence for questioning the entire indulgence theory. Already on 11 November, Luther sent out another copy of his theses (p. 72), this time to his friend John Lang at Erfurt. This was to serve notice to him and to the theologians at Erfurt concerning the Ninety-five Theses. Here, then, we can plainly see that Luther, as he had often said,[29] was sending the theses to learned men of his acquaintance to provoke them to take issue with the theses. Of the other letters that Luther wrote in this connection there is no trace. It is to be assumed, however, that they were sent about the same time. But the letter to Lang is sufficient to refute once more the claim that Luther wrote his theses for perusal to the responsible bishops and that they were not written to evoke a debate. By 11 November, it would have been impossible to have had or to have expected a reply (at that time Cardinal Albert did not even have the letter of 31 October at hand). If Luther sent out copies of his theses on 11 November, then it was because he wanted to make them known among men with whom he hoped to debate them. (Cf. his preface to the theses.)

The letter to Spalatin, which is from the early part of November 1517, is of special importance. Definite conclusions can be drawn from it: Luther answers Spalatin's inquiry why he did not send the Ninety-five Theses to the court. Spalatin, therefore, at least must have heard about the theses by that time and perhaps was already in possession of a copy. Moreover, the theses were already known to a somewhat large circle because Luther speaks of "the many" who assumed that the elector was behind them. If this was the case in the very early part of November, there can be no other explanation than that "the many," just as Spalatin and the court, knew the theses from the posting on the door of the castle chapel from which copies were circulated. In the early days of November—the letter was written, at the latest, on 5 November—such an echo could not have been caused by Luther's private circulation of the theses, even if he had begun this immediately after 31 October. We have no information concerning this. At any rate Spalatin did not receive a copy; it is precisely because of this that he complains.

The letter to the bishop of Brandenburg (pp. 74ff.) once more expressly verifies our theory. At the occasion of sending the manuscript of the *Resolutions*, Luther once more reports to Bishop Jerome concerning developments. This letter to Luther's own bishop a few months after the event is evidence of the first rank that makes it difficult to give serious consideration to the contention that Luther's theses were not at all intended for a debate but merely as a communication to the responsible bishops. To one of the two bishops Luther here states that he wrote the theses exclusively for the purpose of calling for a debate, a debate in which all might participate: "publicly everyone" (through the posting, which is symbolic of the same idea; cf. also the preface to the theses); "personally all whom I knew to be the most learned, that they may write me their opinion" (cf. the letter to Lang and to the theological faculty at Erfurt). The letters to Scheurl (p. 76) and to Trutfetter (p. 77) clarify the events once more, this time in retrospect. The letter to Pope Leo X dated May 1518 (pp. 78ff.) is a dedication of the *Resolutions* of the Ninety-five Theses and characterizes the theses once more. The letter of November 1518 (p. 80) to Frederick the Wise was written at the elector's order and was to serve as a covering letter to the prince's reply to Cardinal Cajetan. In his paragraph about the theses Luther defends his prince against the charge that he had provoked the writing of the theses, actually an unfounded charge (compare the letter on p. 74, which shows how extremely careful Luther had been in his actions). In the contemporary discussion, this letter, like the last one (p. 80), plays a significant role. From this letter, as in the letter of 1 November 1527 to Amsdorf, we reprint only that portion that pertains to the matter of indulgences (respectively, the Ninety-five Theses). The remaining portion of it is not related to our theme. Luther writes first about his own welfare, then about affairs in his home, which has been visited by pestilence. But the sentence with which the letter is dated unquestionably has to be repeated (the text immediately preceding is included only so the final sentence would not appear out of context). It provides the chief support for the theory that the theses were posted not on 31 October but rather on 1 November 1517.[30]

In the fourth section of texts (pp. 81ff.), we present Luther's remarks on our subject given in the transcripts of the so-called Table Talk. In the annotations evidence is discussed in detail and commented on. As a conclusion to the texts there are two reflections of Luther. The one in the preface to his volume of theses composed up to 1538 (pp. 89ff.) should be closely associated with what is said in the first text of our presentation, the autobiographical reflections of 1545. The excerpt from the "Exhortation to the Clergy" of 1530 (pp. 92ff.) is concerned with presenting the changes the Reformation has brought. With its sections on indulgences, repentance, etc., this constitutes a commentary on the

Ninety-five Theses and of their effects, expressed in as moving a manner as could be.

The texts are composed with the principles of the Luther Deutsch edition in mind, that is, they are readable and understandable without further comment. By means of an index in the margins of the pages, readers can check the original texts in the Weimar Edition, the American Edition, and the *Corpus Reformatorum* and quote from them without difficulty. Annotations are limited, therefore, to what seemed to be the minimum number. The book is really presented as a workbook that lets one text interpret another with a continuity of readings and lays before the readers a well-rounded picture and the prerequisite for a personal value judgment. In the annotations, reference is made to contemporary discussions but with conscious restrictions. The problems in the limelight today, it appears to me, will not have lasting validity. It seems apparent, at least, that the contemporary discussion will undergo a change in the foreseeable future. Those who wish to pursue the subject further are asked to turn to the bibliographical section (pp. 101ff.). This section with its occasional indications of content or evaluations is designed for readers who have little time or are only moderately interested in the issues.

This book was produced at the invitation of the publisher. I have taken on the task of editing it because I felt I could not turn away from the opportunity to instruct the church concerning the events of 450 years ago. In 1965, the volume appeared in a German edition produced by Furche-Verlag, Hamburg. President A. O. Fuerbringer of Concordia Seminary (St. Louis) conceived the idea of producing an edition in the English language. For this new edition I have reviewed especially the introduction and the notes once more and have incorporated the results of my own work as well as of continuing discussions since 1965. I am indebted and sincerely thankful to President Fuerbringer, to his colleagues of Concordia Seminary, to the Foundation for Reformation Research, and to the staff of Concordia Publishing House, who cooperated in this work.

Kurt Aland
Münster, Germany
18 February 1967
The Day of Luther's Death

TEXTS

I

The Prehistory of the Ninety-five Theses and Their Connection with the History of the Reformation

LUTHER'S PREFACE TO VOLUME 1 OF HIS LATIN WRITINGS, WITTENBERG EDITION, 1545

Martin Luther wishes the sincere reader salvation!

WA 54:179

For a long time I strenuously resisted those who wanted my books, or more correctly my confused lucubrations, published. I did LW 34:327 not want the labors of the ancients to be buried by my new works and the reader kept from reading them. Then, too, by God's grace a great many systematic books now exist, among which the *Loci communes* of Philip [Melanchthon] excel, with which a theologian and a bishop can be beautifully and abundantly prepared to be mighty in preaching the doctrine of piety, especially since the Holy Bible itself can now be had in nearly every language. But my books, as it happened, yes, as the lack of order in which the events transpired made it necessary, are accordingly crude and disordered chaos, which is now not easy to arrange even for me.

Persuaded by these reasons, I wished that all my books were buried in perpetual oblivion, so that there might be room for better

328 ones. But the boldness and bothersome perseverance of others daily filled my ears with complaints that it would come to pass, that if I did not permit their publication in my lifetime, men wholly ignorant of the causes and the time of the events would nevertheless most certainly publish them, and so out of one confusion many would arise. Their boldness, I say, prevailed and so I permitted them to be published. At the same time the wish and command of our most illustrious Prince, Elector, etc., John Frederick was added. He commanded, yes, compelled the printers not only to print, but to speed up the publication.[1]

But above all else, I beg the sincere reader, and I beg for the sake of our Lord Jesus Christ himself, to read those things judiciously, yes, with great commiseration. May he be mindful of the fact that I was once a monk and a most enthusiastic papist when I began that cause. I was so drunk, yes, submerged in the pope's dogmas, that I would have been ready to murder all, if I could have, or to co-operate willingly with the murderers of all who would take but a syllable from obedience to the pope. So great a Saul was I, as are many to this day. I was not such a lump of frigid ice in defending the papacy as Eck and his like were, who appeared to me actually to defend the pope more for their own belly's sake than to pursue the matter seriously. To me, indeed, they seem to laugh at the pope to this day, like Epicureans! I pursued the matter with all seriousness, as one, who in dread of the last day, nevertheless from the depth of my heart wanted to be saved.

So you will find how much and what important matters I humbly conceded to the pope in my earlier writings, which I later and now hold and execrate as the worst blasphemies and abomination. You 180 will, therefore, sincere reader, ascribe this error, or, as they slander, contradiction to the time and my inexperience. At first I was all alone and certainly very inept and unskilled in conducting such great affairs. For I got into these turmoils by accident and not by will or intention. I call upon God himself as witness.

329 Hence, when in the year 1517 indulgences were sold (I wanted to say promoted) in these regions for most shameful gain—I was then a preacher, a young doctor of theology, so to speak—and I began to dissuade the people and to urge them not to listen to the clamors of the indulgence hawkers; they had better things to do. I certainly thought

that in this case I should have a protector in the pope, on whose trust-worthiness I then leaned strongly, for in his decrees he most clearly damned the immoderation of the quaestors, as he called the indulgence preachers.

Soon afterward I wrote two letters, one to Albrecht, the archbishop of Mainz,[2] who got half of the money from the indulgences, the pope the other half—something I did not know at the time—the other to the ordinary (as they call them) Jerome, the bishop of Brandenburg.[3] I begged them to stop the shameless blasphemy of the quaestors. But the poor little brother was despised. Despised, I published the *Theses*[4] and at the same time a German *Sermon on Indulgences*,[5] shortly thereafter also the *Explanations* [*Resolutions*], in which, to the pope's honor, I developed the idea that indulgences should indeed not be condemned, but that good works of love should be preferred to them.[6] 330

This was demolishing heaven and consuming the earth with fire. I am accused by the pope, am cited to Rome, and the whole papacy rises up against me alone. All this happened in the year 1518, when Maximilian held the diet at Augsburg. In it, Cardinal Cajetan served as the pope's Lateran legate. The most illustrious Duke Frederick of Saxony, Elector Prince, approached him on my behalf and brought it about that I was not compelled to go to Rome, but that he himself should summon me to examine and compose the matter. Soon the diet adjourned. 181

The Germans in the meantime, all tired of suffering the pillagings, traffickings, and endless impostures of Roman rascals, awaited with bated breath the outcome of so great a matter, which no one before, neither bishop nor theologian, had dared to touch. In any case that popular breeze favored me, because those practices and "Romanations," with which they had filled and tired the whole earth, were already hateful to all.

So I came to Augsburg, afoot and poor, supplied with food and letters of commendation from Prince Frederick to the senate and to certain good men. I was there three days before I went to the cardinal, though he cited me day by day through a certain orator, for those excellent men forbade and dissuaded me most strenuously, not to go to the cardinal without a safe conduct from the emperor. The orator 331 was rather troublesome to me, urging that if I should only revoke, everything would be all right! But as great as the wrong, so long is the detour to its correction.

Finally, on the third day he came demanding to know why I did not come to the cardinal, who expected me most benignly. I replied that I had to respect the advice of those very fine men to whom I had been commended by Prince Frederick, but it was their advice by no means to go to the cardinal without the emperor's protection or safe conduct. Having obtained this (but they took action on the part of the imperial senate to obtain it), I would come at once. At this point he blew up. "What?" he said, "Do you suppose Prince Frederick will take up arms for your sake?" I said, "This I do not at all desire." "And where will you stay?" I replied, "Under heaven." Then he, "If you had the pope and the cardinals in your power, what would you do?" "I would," said I, "show them all respect and honor." Thereupon he, wagging his finger with an Italian gesture, said, "Hem!" And so he left, nor did he return.

182 On that day the imperial senate informed the cardinal that the emperor's protection or a safe conduct had been granted me and admonished him that he should not design anything too severe against me. He is said to have replied, "It is well. I shall nevertheless do whatever my duty demands." These things were the start of that tumult. The rest can be learned from the accounts included later.

332 Master Philip Melanchthon had already been called here that same year by Prince Frederick to teach Greek literature,[7] doubtless so that I should have an associate in the work of theology. His works attest sufficiently what the Lord has performed through this instrument, not only in literature but also in theology, though Satan is mad and all his adherents.

Maximilian died, in the following year, [15]19, in February,[8] and according to the law of the empire Duke Frederick was made deputy. Thereupon the storm ceased to rage a bit, and gradually contempt of excommunication or papal thunderbolts arose. For when Eck and Caraccioli brought a bull from Rome condemning Luther and revealed it,[9] the former here, the latter there to Duke Frederick, who was at Cologne at the time together with other princes in order to meet Charles who had been recently elected, Frederick was most indignant. He reproved that papal rascal with great courage and constancy, because in his absence he and Eck had disturbed his and his brother John's dominion. He jarred them so magnificently that they left him in shame and disgrace. The prince, endowed with incredible insight, caught on to the devices of the Roman Curia and knew how to deal with them in a becoming manner, for he had a keen nose and smelled more and farther than the Romanists could hope or fear.

Hence they refrained from putting him to a test. For he did not dignify with the least respect the Rose, which they call "golden," sent him that same year[10] by Leo X, indeed ridiculed it. So the Romanists were forced to despair of their attempts to deceive so great a prince. The gospel advanced happily under the shadow of that prince and was widely propagated. His authority influenced very many, for since he was a very wise and most keen-sighted prince, he could incur the sus- 333 picion only among the hateful that he wanted to nourish and protect heresy and heretics. This did the papacy great harm.

That same year the Leipzig debate was held,[11] to which Eck had 183 challenged us two, Karlstadt and me. But I could not, in spite of all my letters, get a safe conduct from Duke George. Accordingly, I came to Leipzig not as a prospective debater, but as a spectator under the safe conduct granted to Karlstadt. Who stood in my way I do not know, for till then Duke George was not against me. This I know for certain.

Here Eck came to me in my lodging and said he had heard that I refused to debate. I replied, "How can I debate, since I cannot get a safe conduct from Duke George?" "If I cannot debate with you," he said, "neither do I want to with Karlstadt, for I have come here on your account. What if I obtain a safe conduct for you? Would you then debate with me?" "Obtain," said I, "and it shall be." He left and soon a safe conduct was given me too and the opportunity to debate.

Eck did this because he discerned the certain glory that was set before him on account of my proposition in which I denied that the pope is the head of the church by divine right. Here a wide field was open to him and a supreme occasion to flatter in praiseworthy manner the pope and to merit his favor, also to ruin me with hate and envy. He did this vigorously throughout the entire debate. But he neither proved his own position nor refuted mine, so that even Duke George said to Eck and me at the morning meal, "Whether he be pope by human or divine right, yet he is pope." He would in no case have said this had he not been influenced by the arguments, but would have approved of Eck only.

Here, in my case, you may also see how hard it is to struggle out of and emerge from errors which have been confirmed by the example of the whole world and have by long habit become a part of nature, as it were. How true is the proverb, "It is hard to give up the accustomed," and, "Custom is second nature." How truly Augustine says, "If one does not resist custom, it becomes a necessity." I had then already read and taught the sacred Scriptures most diligently privately and publicly for seven years, so that I knew them nearly all by memory. I had also acquired the beginning of the knowledge of Christ and faith in him, i.e., not by works but by faith in Christ are we made righteous and saved. Finally, regarding that of which I speak, I had already defended the proposition publicly that the pope is not the head of the church by divine right. Nevertheless, I did not draw the conclusion, namely, that the pope must be of the devil. For what is not of God must of necessity be of the devil.

So absorbed was I, as I have said, by the example and the title of the holy church as well as by my own habit, that I conceded human right to the pope, which nevertheless, unless it is founded on divine authority, is a diabolical lie. For we obey parents and magistrates not because they themselves command it, but because it is God's will, I Peter 3 [2:13]. For that reason I can bear with a less hateful spirit those who cling too pertinaciously to the papacy, particularly those who have not read the sacred Scriptures, or also the profane, since I, who read the sacred Scriptures most diligently so many years, still clung to it so tenaciously.

In the year 1519, Leo X, as I have said, sent the Rose with Karl von Miltitz, who urged me profusely to be reconciled with the pope.[12] He had seventy apostolic briefs that if Prince Frederick would turn me over to him, as the pope requested by means of the Rose, he should tack one up in each city and so transfer me safely to Rome. But he betrayed the counsel of his heart toward me when he said, "O Martin, I believed you were some aged theologian who, sitting behind the stove, disputed thus with himself; now I see you are still young and strong. If I had twenty-five thousand armed men, I do not believe I could take you to Rome, for I have sounded out the people's mind all along the way to learn what they thought of you. Behold, where I found one standing for the pope, three stood for you against the pope." But that was ridiculous! He had also asked simple little women and girls in the hostelries, what they thought of the Roman chair. Ignorant of this term and thinking of a domestic chair, they replied, "How can we know what kind of chairs you have in Rome, wood or stone?"

Therefore he begged me to seek the things which made for peace. He would put forth every effort to have the pope do the same. I also promised everything abundantly. Whatever I could do with a good conscience with respect to the truth, I would do most promptly. I, too, desired and was eager for peace. Having been drawn into these disturbances by force and driven by necessity, I had done all I did: the guilt was not mine.

But he had summoned Johann Tetzel of the preaching order, the primary author of this tragedy, and had with verbose threats from the pope so broken the man, till then so terrible to all, a fearless crier, that from that time on he wasted away and was finally consumed by illness of mind. When I found this out before his death, I comforted him with a letter,[13] written benignly, asking him to be of good cheer and not to fear my memory. But perhaps he succumbed a victim of his 336 conscience and of the pope's indignation.

Karl von Miltitz was regarded as vain and his advice as vain. But, 185 in my opinion, if the man at Mainz had from the start, when I admonished him, and, finally, if the pope, before he condemned me unheard and raged with his bulls, had taken this advice, which Karl took although too late, and had at once quenched Tetzel's fury, the matter would not have come to so great a tumult. The entire guilt belongs to the one at Mainz, whose smartness and cleverness fooled him, with which he wanted to suppress my doctrine and have his money, acquired by the indulgences, saved. Now counsels are sought in vain; in vain efforts are made. The Lord has awakened and stands to judge the people. [Cf. Dan. 9:14.] Though they could kill us, they still do not have what they want, yes, have less than they have, while we live in safety. This some of them who are not entirely of a dull nose smell quite enough.

Meanwhile, I had already during that year returned to interpret the Psalter anew.[14] I had confidence in the fact that I was more skilful, after I had lectured in the university on St. Paul's epistles to the Romans,[15] to the Galatians,[16] and the one to the Hebrews.[17] I had indeed been captivated with an extraordinary ardor for understanding Paul in the Epistle to the Romans. But up till then it was not the cold blood about the heart, but a single word in Chapter 1[:17], "In it the righteousness of God is revealed," that had stood in my way. For I hated that word "righteousness of God," which, according to the use and custom of all the teachers, I had been taught to understand philosophically regarding the formal or active righteousness, as they called it, with which God is righteous and punishes the unrighteous sinner.

Though I lived as a monk without reproach, I felt that I was a sinner before God with an extremely disturbed conscience. I could not believe that he was placated by my satisfaction. I did not love, yes, I 337 hated the righteous God who punishes sinners, and secretly, if not blasphemously, certainly murmuring greatly, I was angry with God, and said, "As if, indeed, it is not enough, that miserable sinners, eternally lost through original sin, are crushed by every kind of calamity by the law of the decalogue, without having God add pain to pain by the gospel and also by the gospel threatening us with his righteousness 186 and wrath!" Thus I raged with a fierce and troubled conscience. Nevertheless, I beat importunately upon Paul at that place, most ardently desiring to know what St. Paul wanted.

At last, by the mercy of God, meditating day and night, I gave heed to the context of the words, namely, "In it the righteousness of God is revealed, as it is written, 'He who through faith is righteous shall live.' " There I began to understand that the righteousness of God is that by which the righteous lives by a gift of God, namely by faith. And this is the meaning: the righteousness of God is revealed by the gospel, namely, the passive righteousness with which merciful God justifies us by faith, as it is written, "He who through faith is righteous shall live." Here I felt that I was altogether born again and had entered paradise itself through open gates. There a totally other face of the entire Scripture showed itself to me. Thereupon I ran through the Scriptures from memory. I also found in other terms an analogy, as, the work of God, that is, what God does in us, the power of God, with which he makes us strong, the wisdom of God, with which he makes us wise, the strength of God, the salvation of God, the glory of God.

And I extolled my sweetest word with a love as great as the hatred with which I had before hated the word "righteousness of God." Thus that place in Paul was for me truly the gate to paradise. Later I read Augustine's *The Spirit and the Letter*,[18] where contrary to hope I found that he, too, interpreted God's righteousness in a similar way, as the righteousness with which God clothes us when he justifies us. Although this was heretofore said imperfectly and he did not explain all things concerning imputation clearly, it nevertheless was pleasing that God's righteousness with which we are justified was taught. Armed more fully with these thoughts, I began a second time to interpret the Psalter. And the work would have grown into a large commentary, if I had not again been compelled to leave the work begun, 338 because Emperor Charles V in the following year convened the diet at Worms.[19]

I relate these things, good reader, so that, if you are a reader of my puny works, you may keep in mind, that, as I said above, I was all alone and one of those who, as Augustine says of himself, have become proficient by writing and teaching. I was not one of those who from nothing suddenly become the topmost, though they are nothing, neither have labored, nor been tempted, nor become experienced, but have with one look at the Scriptures exhausted their entire spirit.

To this point, to the year 1520 and 21, the indulgence matter proceeded. Upon that followed the sacramentarian and the Anabaptist 187 affairs. Regarding these a preface shall be written to other tomes, if I live.

Farewell in the Lord, reader, and pray for the growth of the Word against Satan. Strong and evil, now also very furious and savage, he knows his time is short and the kingdom of his pope is in danger. But may God confirm in us what he has accomplished and perfect his work which he began in us, to his glory. Amen.

March 5, in the year 1545.

"AGAINST HANSWURST, 1541"

WA 51:538 Since he [Albert of Mainz][20] does not want to know who caused this
Lutheran rumpus[21] (as he calls it) I will announce it publicly, and not
LW 41:231 just to Harry[22] or to him, for he knows it much better than I do. It
happened, in the year 1517, that a preaching monk called John Tetzel,
a great ranter, made his appearance. He had previously been rescued
in Innsbruck by Duke Frederick from a sack—for Maximilian had
condemned him to be drowned in the Inn (presumably on account of
his great virtue)—and Duke Frederick reminded him of it when he
began to slander us Wittenbergers; he also freely admitted it himself.
This same Tetzel now went around with indulgences, selling grace for
money as dearly or as cheaply as he could, to the best of his ability. At
539 that time I was a preacher here in the monastery, and a fledgling doctor[23] fervent and enthusiastic for Holy Scripture.

Now when many people from Wittenberg went to Jütterbock and
Zerbst for indulgences, and I (as truly as my Lord Christ redeemed
232 me) did not know what the indulgences were, as in fact no one knew,
I began to preach very gently that one could probably do something
better and more reliable than acquiring indulgences. I had also
preached before in the same way against indulgences at the castle[24]
and had thus gained the disfavor of Duke Frederick because he was
very fond of his religious foundation. Now I—to point out the true
cause of the Lutheran rumpus—let everything take its course. However, I heard what dreadful and abominable articles Tetzel was preaching, and some of them I shall mention now, namely:

That he had such grace and power from the pope that even if
someone seduced the holy Virgin Mary, and made her conceive, he
could forgive him, provided he placed the necessary sum in the box.

Again, that the red indulgence-cross, bearing the papal arms, was
when erected in church as powerful as the cross of Christ.

Again, that if St. Peter were here now, he would not have greater
grace or power than he had.

Again, that he would not change places with St. Peter in heaven,
for he had rescued more souls with indulgences than St. Peter had
with his preaching.

Again, that if anyone put money in the box for a soul in purgatory, the soul would fly to heaven as soon as the coin clinked on the bottom.

Again, that the grace from indulgences was the same grace as that by which a man is reconciled to God.

Again, that it was not necessary to have remorse, sorrow, or repentance for sin, if one bought (I ought to say, acquired) an indulgence or a dispensation; indeed, he sold also for future sin.

He did an abominable amount of this, and it was all for the sake of money. I did not know at that time who would get the money. Then a booklet appeared, magnificently ornamented with the coat of arms of the bishop of Magdeburg, in which the sellers of indulgences were advised to preach some of these articles.[25] It became quite evident that Bishop Albrecht had hired this Tetzel because he was a great ranter; for he was elected bishop of Mainz with the agreement that he was himself to buy (I mean acquire) the pallium at Rome. For three bishops of Mainz, Berthold, Jakob, and Uriel, had recently died, one shortly after the other, so that it was perhaps difficult for the diocese to buy the pallium so often and in such quick succession, since it cost twenty-six thousand gulden according to some, and thirty thousand according to others, for the most holy father of Rome can charge as much as that for flax (which otherwise is hardly worth six cents).

Thus the bishop devised this scheme, hoping to pay the Fuggers (for they had advanced the money for the pallium) from the purse of the common man. And he sent this great fleecer of men's pockets into the provinces; he fleeced them so thoroughly that a pile of money began to come clinking and clattering into the boxes. He did not forget himself in this either. And in addition the pope had a finger in the pie as well, because one-half was to go toward the building of St. Peter's Church in Rome. Thus these fellows went about their work joyfully and full of hope, rattling their boxes under men's purses and fleecing them. But, as I say, I did not know that at the time.

Then I wrote a letter with the *Theses* to the bishop of Magdeburg,[26] admonishing and beseeching him to stop Tetzel and prevent this stupid thing from being preached, lest it give rise to public discontent—this was a proper thing for him to do as archbishop. I can still lay my hands on that letter; but I never received an answer. I

233

540

234 wrote in the same manner to the bishop of Brandenburg as my ordinary; in him I had a very gracious bishop. He answered that I was attacking the authority of the church and would get myself into trouble. He advised me to leave it alone.[27] I can well imagine that they both thought the pope would be much too powerful for me, a miserable beggar.

So my theses against Tetzel's articles, which you can now see in print, were published. They went throughout the whole of Germany in a fortnight, for the whole world complained about indulgences, and particularly about Tetzel's articles. And because all the bishops and doctors were silent and no one wanted to bell the cat (for the masters of heresy, the preaching order,[28] had instilled fear into the

541 whole world with the threat of fire, and Tetzel had bullied a number of priests who had grumbled against his impudent preaching), Luther became famous as a doctor, for at last someone had stood up to fight. I did not want the fame, because (as I have said) I did not myself know what the indulgences were, and the song might prove too high for my voice.

This is the first, real, fundamental beginning of the Lutheran rumpus.

—⟶⟵—

542 The other cause for the beginning of this rumpus was the most
235 holy father, Pope Leo, with his untimely ban. Doctor Sow[29] and all the papists helped him with it, as did a number of silly asses, indeed, everyone who wanted to win his spurs at my expense. They wrote and ranted against me, that is, whoever could hold a pen in his hand.
543 But I hoped the pope would protect me because I had so secured and armed my disputation with Scripture and papal decretals[30] that I was sure the pope would damn Tetzel and bless me. I also dedicated the *Explanations* to him with a humble essay,[31] and this book of mine greatly pleased even many cardinals and bishops. For I was at that time a better papist than Mainz[32] and Harry have ever been, or could possibly be, and the papal decretals say quite clearly that indulgence sellers cannot redeem souls from purgatory with indulgences. But while I waited for the blessing from Rome, thunder and lightning

came. I had to be the sheep who troubled the water for the wolf. Tetzel went free, but I had to be eaten.

In addition, they treated me in such a fine popish way that I was, to be sure, damned in Rome sixteen days before the citation came to me.[33] But when Cardinal Cajetan came to the diet in Augsburg, Dr. Staupitz arranged for that same good prince, Duke Frederick, to go to the cardinal and obtain a hearing with him for me. Thus I came to the cardinal in Augsburg. He himself appeared friendly, and after much discussion I offered to be silent thereafter, if my opponents would also be compelled to be silent. Since I did not succeed in that, I went from pope to council,[34] and left. Thus the matter came before the diet, and was often discussed there—but I cannot write about that now since it is too long a story. In the meantime there have been written exchanges of the most violent kind, until the point is now reached that they unashamedly avoid the light, indeed, they now teach many things that formerly they damned. Moreover, they would have had nothing to teach if our books had not existed. 236

Now if a rumpus has arisen out of this which causes them pain, they have only themselves to thank. Why did they handle matters so imprudently and clumsily, contrary to all justice and truth, and contrary to Scripture and their own decretals? They should blame no one except themselves. We, however, shall laugh up our sleeves at their complaints and ridicule them, and console ourselves that their hour has come. Even now they still deal with the matter like blind, hardened, senseless fools, as if they wilfully desired to perish. God's wrath has come upon them as they have deserved. 545

For now (God be praised) that it has become evident how devilish a lie indulgences are, they do not repent or think of improving or reforming themselves; but with that simple word "church" they want blindly to defend all their abominations. And if they had done nothing else wrong, these indulgences would be enough for God to damn them to the fires of hell, and for all men to drive them from the world. Just think, dear Christian, how, first, the pope, the cardinals, the bishops, and all the clergy have filled and deceived the world with these lying indulgences; second, how they have blasphemously called them the grace of God, though they are and can be nothing except a remission of satisfaction,[35] that is, nothing. For we know now that satisfac- 237

43

tion is nothing. Third, think how they have, with abominable simony[36] and Iscariotry,[37] sold them for money as the grace of God, whereas God's grace must be given freely [Matt. 10:8]. Fourth, think how they have taken and stolen money and property from the whole world—and all in the name of God. Fifth, and worst of all, think how 546 they have made these blasphemous lies into a terrible idolatry. Many thousands of souls who have died relying on them as though they were God's grace are lost because of these murderers of men's souls, since whoever trusts and builds on lies is a servant of the devil.

Such souls eternally scream their verdict over the papacy, which ought to reinstate them before God. Moreover, they ought to give back all the money and property they stole. Above all, they ought to restore to God his honor, of which they shamefully robbed him with their indulgences. When will they do that? When indeed will they care about it? But if they will not do it, by what pretense would they call themselves a Christian church, and possess or demand church property? Should that be called a church which, as we have seen, is full of indulgences, that is, of devilish lies, idolatry, simony, Iscariotry, robbery, and the murder of souls? Well then, whether they like it or not, they must. He is strong enough to wrest it from them, at any rate, with the eternal fires of hell. Meanwhile they ought not to be or to be called a church, but a synagogue of the devil [Rev. 2:9], even if all the Harrys and Mainzes rage and foam at the mouth about it.

MELANCHTHON'S PREFACE TO VOLUME 2 OF LUTHER'S LATIN WRITINGS, WITTENBERG EDITION, 1546

CR 6:155   Martin Luther, whom we all respect, had given us reason to hope that in this part of his written works he would relate the course of his life and the occasions of his conflicts.[38] This he would have done if the author had not been summoned from this mortal life to the eternal fellowship of God and the church in heaven before the printing works had completed this volume. And a comprehensive written account of his private life would have been useful, for it was full of examples 156 that would have been of service for the establishment of piety in the hearts of good men. The report on the occasions of his conflicts could also have reminded posterity of many matters. Then, too, it could refute the slanders of those who invent the fiction that he was either incited by the princes or others to overthrow the authority of the bishops or that he broke the bonds of monastic servitude inflamed by personal lust. It would have been profitable if these matters had been set forth and related by him in a complete manner and at length. For although malevolent men hurl the common reproach at him that "he blows his own horn," we still know that there was such integrity in him that he would have related his history with the greatest reliability. Many wise men are also still alive to whom the actual course of these events is known, and it would have been ridiculous to invent another history, as is sometimes done in poems.[39] But because the day of his death preceded the publication of this volume, we shall in good faith relate in part what we have heard from him personally and in part what we have seen for ourselves concerning these same matters.[40]

There is an old widely scattered family of middle-class men named Luther under the dominion of the illustrious counts of Mansfeld. But the parents of Martin Luther had their home first of all in the town of Eisleben, where Martin Luther was born. Then they moved to the town of Mansfeld, where his father, John Luther, held offices and was highly esteemed by all good men for his integrity. In his mother, Margaret, the wife of John Luther, in addition to the other virtues which were becoming in an honorable matron, modesty, the fear of God, and prayer were especially conspicuous, and other honorable women looked upon her as an example of virtues. To several inquiries about the time when her son was born she gave me the reply that she remembered the day and the hour for certain but had doubts about the year. She maintained, moreover, that he was born on 10 November during the night after eleven and that the name Martin was assigned to the infant because the following day, on which the child was engrafted into the church of God by baptism, was St. Martin's day. But his brother James, an honorable and reliable man, used to say that it was a family opinion regarding his brother's age that he was born in the year 1483 after Christ's birth.[41]

After he reached the age when he was capable of receiving instruction, his parents carefully accustomed their son Martin by home training to the knowledge and fear of God and the duties involved in the other virtues. And as is customary among honorable men, they took care to teach him reading and writing. The father of George Oehmler [Nicolaus Oehmler] carried him to the elementary school while he was still a small boy. Since he is still alive, he can be a witness of this account. At this time, however, the grammar schools in Saxon towns enjoyed only a moderate fame. For this reason, on reaching the age of 14, Martin was sent to Magdeburg with John Reinecke, whose influence later on was outstanding and who won great respect in these regions by his ability. Between these two men, Luther and Reinecke, mutual goodwill of a high order always prevailed, either because of a kind of natural compatibility or from this association in their boyhood studies. But Luther did not stay longer than a year at Magdeburg. Next for a period of four years at the school at Eisenach he studied under a teacher who taught grammar more correctly and skillfully than it was taught elsewhere. I remember this man's ability being praised by Luther. Moreover, he was sent to this city because his mother descended from an old and honorable family in these parts. Here he finished his studies in grammar. Because the power of his intellect was very keen and especially suitable for eloquence, he quickly outdistanced his fellows and easily surpassed the other youths who were studying with him both in his use of words and fullness of speech and in writing both prose and verse.

After he had tasted of the sweetness of letters, his nature burned with a desire for learning and yearned for the university as the foundation of all instruction. And such a great force of genius could have grasped all the arts in turn if it had found suitable teachers. Perhaps the mellower studies of pure philosophy and care in composing discourse would have been profitable to calm the vehemence of his nature. But it was his fortune in Erfurt to happen upon the rather thorny dialectic of that age. This he quickly grasped because with his keenness of intellect he perceived better than others the causes and sources of the instructions. Since his mind was greedy for learning and demanded more and better things, he himself read most of the classics of the ancient Latin authors: Cicero, Virgil, Livy, and others. There he read not like boys who only pick out the words but as instruction on human living and as pictures of life. Therefore, he also looked more closely both at the counsels and opinions of these writers, and because he had a reliable and firm memory, most of the things he read and heard were always at his ready disposal. In his youth, then, Luther was so prominent that his talents were an object of admiration to the whole university. Accordingly he was awarded the degree of master of philosophy, and when he was 20, he began the study of law on the advice of his relatives. They thought that this great power of intellect and eloquence should be brought to light and be made available for the common good. But shortly afterwards, when he was 21, suddenly and contrary to the expectation of his parents and relatives, he went to the convent of the Augustinian monks at Erfurt and begged to be received. When he was received, he not only learned the doctrine of the church with the greatest of zeal but also controlled himself with the utmost strictness of discipline. And in all the exercises of reading, disputations, fastings, and prayers he surpassed all by far. His nature was such that I was often amazed. Although he was neither small nor weak in body, he was very moderate in food and drink. I have seen him for four days on end, when he was quite well, eating and drinking nothing at all. At other times, I often saw him for many days quite content with a little bit of bread and herring daily.

158

The occasion for entering upon this kind of life which he thought more fitting for piety and studies on the doctrine of God, as he himself used to say, and as many know, was this. Often as he thought more carefully about the wrath of God or extraordinary examples of punishments, such great terrors suddenly struck him that he almost lost consciousness. I myself have seen him when he was overwhelmed by the tension in a doctrinal dispute throw himself on a bed in a neighboring room, where he frequently repeated this statement mingled with prayer: "He has concluded all men under sin, that he may have pity on all" (Romans 11:32). These terrors he experienced either for the first time or most keenly in that year when he lost a companion who was killed by some kind of accident. Therefore, it was not poverty but zeal for piety that led him into this type of monastic life. Although he daily learned the teaching customary here in the schools and read the commentaries on the *Sentences* and in public disputations gave clear explanations of labyrinths inextricable to others, thereby winning the admiration of many, nevertheless, because he was not seeking fame of intellect but nourishment for piety in this kind of life, he treated these studies as sidelines and easily laid hold of these scholastic methods. In the meantime he eagerly read the sources of heavenly doctrine, the prophetic and apostolic Scriptures, so that he might instruct his heart on the will of God and nurture fear and 159 trust in God with firm testimonies. He was moved by his own griefs and terrors to pursue this study more intensively. He used to tell us that he was often strengthened by the sermons of a certain old man in the Augustinian monastery at Erfurt. When he told this man what it was that alarmed him, he heard him discoursing at length on faith, and he used to say that he was led to the creed, in which we read: "I believe the remission of sins." This article he interpreted to mean that it should not only be believed in general that some men are forgiven, as the demons also believe that David and Peter are forgiven, but that it is God's command that each and every one of us should believe that our sins are forgiven us. This interpretation, he said, was confirmed by a saying of Bernhard, and a passage from a sermon on the Annunciation was shown him which contained these words: "But add that you should believe also this, that through Him sins are also forgiven TO YOU. This is the testimony which the Holy Spirit gives in your heart saying: 'Your sins are forgiven you.' It is also the view of the apostle that a man is justified freely through faith" [*MPL*, 183, 384].

Luther used to say that he had not only been strengthened by this word but had also been reminded of the whole position of St. Paul, who so often emphasized this phrase: We are justified by faith. Although he had read the explanations of many men concerning this phrase, he had then, from the sermons of this man and the consolation imparted to his heart, learned to know the vanity of the interpretations he then had in hand. Gradually more light came to him as he read and compared the statements and examples recounted in the prophets and apostles and stimulated his faith by daily prayer. Then he also began to read the books of St. Augustine, where he found many clear statements in his explanation of the Psalms and in the book *On the Spirit and the Letter,* and these confirmed this doctrine concerning faith and the consolation that had been kindled in his own heart. But he did not yet give up the commentaries on the *Sen-*

tences completely, and he could recite Gabriel Biel and Pierre d'Ailly almost word for word from memory. Long and often did he read the works of William Occam, for he preferred his acuteness to that of Thomas Aquinas and John Duns Scotus. He had also read John Gerson diligently. But Augustine's works he had often read in their entirety, and he had thoroughly memorized their content. This very severe course of study he began at Erfurt, and he stayed at the Augustinian convent of this city for four years.

160

At this time, moreover, Staupitz, who deserves our highest respect and who had assisted at the founding of the University of Wittenberg, desired to promote the study of theology in the newly founded academy there. When he noted the ability and learning of Luther, he transferred him to Wittenberg in 1508. Luther was now 26. Here in the midst of his daily employments in the school and in preaching, his gifts began to shine forth even more. And when men gifted with wisdom, Dr. Martin Mellerstadt among others, listened to him with attention, Mellerstadt often said that there were such great gifts in this man that he had a clear premonition that he would change the common method of teaching, which was then the only method handed down in the schools.

At first he lectured on the *Dialectics* and *Physics* of Aristotle. In the meantime, however, he did not lay aside his zeal for reading theological writings. After three years he journeyed to Rome because of controversies among the monks. He returned in the same year and according to the customary procedure of the schools was decorated with a doctor's degree, as we usually say. The duke of Saxony, Elector Frederick, bore the expenses. He had heard Luther preaching and admired his force of spirit and the power of his oratory and the good subject matter set forth in his sermons. And that you may see that the doctor's degree was bestowed on him with a kind of maturity and judgment, so to say, you should know that this was the 30th year of Luther's life. He himself used to tell us that he had been very reluctant and unwilling when instructed by Staupitz to allow himself to be decorated with this degree and that Staupitz had said jokingly that God would have plenty of work in his church for which Luther's services would be useful. Although these words were spoken in jest, the outcome was in agreement with this statement, even as many premonitions precede changes.

Later he began to lecture on the Epistle to the Romans and then on the Psalms. These writings he explained in such a manner that, in the judgment of all godly and wise men, a light of new doctrine seemed to arise after a long and dark night. Here he demonstrated the distinction between the Law and the Gospel; here he refuted the error which then reigned in the schools and sermons, which teaches that men merit the remission of sins by their own works and that men are just before God by means of discipline, as the Pharisees taught. Luther, accordingly, recalled the hearts of men to the Son of God and like the Baptist pointed out the Lamb of God who has borne our sins. He showed that sins are forgiven freely on account of God's Son and that this blessing, to be sure, must be accepted by faith. He also explained other parts of ecclesiastical doctrine. These excellent beginnings invested him with great authority, especially because the ethics of the teacher agreed with what he said. It seemed that his speech did not come from his lips but from his heart. Admiration for this kind of life wakened strong favor for him in the hearts of his hearers, as the ancients also said, "Generally speaking, they say, good behavior produces the most commanding respect." For this reason, when he later on changed certain rites, honorable men who knew him were less vehemently opposed to him. Because of the authority he had previously gained by his presentation of matters of importance and by the sanctity of his life, they agreed with him in these matters of opinion by which they saw the world being torn asunder to their great grief.

But at that time Luther did not bring about any change in the matter of rites. He was a rather stern guardian of discipline in his circle, and he did not bring in any admixture of more frightening opinions. But to all men he explained ever more clearly the doctrine that was common and absolutely necessary, concerning repentance, concerning the remission of sins, concerning faith, and concerning true consolation in tribulation. All godly men were really taken captive by the sweetness of this doctrine. The learned men, moreover, welcomed the fact that Christ, the prophets, and the apostles were being brought forth from darkness, prison, and squalor, so to say. The distinction between the Law and the Gospel, between the promise of the Law and the promise of the Gospel, between philosophy and the Gospel, between spiritual righteousness and political factors was being recognized, something that was certainly not prominent in Thomas, Scotus, and the like. There was also the additional factor that the studies of young men had already been directed to the learning of the Latin and Greek languages by the writings of Erasmus. For this reason, after they were shown a sweeter kind of doctrine, many who were endowed with a good and open understanding began to recoil in horror from the barbarous and sophistical doctrine of the monks. Luther himself also began to devote himself to the study of the Greek and Hebrew languages, so that after he had learned the peculiar idiomatic nature of the language and had drawn doctrine from the sources, he might be in a position to make a more correct judgment.

While Luther was at this stage of his life, indulgences were being hawked for sale in these parts by a most impudent Dominican sycophant, Tetzel. Irritated by this man's impious and wicked sermons and burning with zeal for godliness, Luther published his *Propositions* [*Theses*] *on Indulgences*, which are found in the first volume of his writings [that is, the Wittenberg Edition of the Latin writings]. These he nailed up in public to the church that is near the castle at Wittenberg on the day before the festival of All Saints in the year 1517 [that is, 31 October]. Now Tetzel remained true to character and also hoped to earn thanks from the pope at Rome. He convened his senate, several monks and theologians who were colored however lightly by his sophistry. He ordered them to write something against Luther. In the meantime, so as not to become merely a dumb character, he now hurled against Luther not sermons but thunderbolts. Everywhere he raised the shout that this heretic should be burned, and he also publicly hurled into the flames Luther's theses and also his sermon on indulgences. These acts of madness on the part of Tetzel and his satellites imposed on Luther the necessity of discoursing on these same matters at greater length and of defending the truth.

These were the beginnings of this controversy, in which no thought or dream of any future change in rites even entered Luther's mind. He did not even completely cast off indulgences but only demanded moderation. Therefore, he is falsely charged by those who say that he began matters from a plausible cause, so that he might

162

later on change the state and seek power either for himself or for others. He was so far from being suborned and incited by courtiers, as the duke of Braunschweig wrote,[42] that it actually grieved Duke Frederick that conflicts were being stirred up. Looking ahead, he saw that even though the beginning might be a matter of plausible concern, this flame would gradually spread wider, as is said in Homer concerning strife: "Small at first, it soon raises itself to the skies" (*Iliad* iv, 442). And because Frederick, over and above all princes of our age, was an avid lover of public peace and in no sense a covetous man and was especially accustomed to direct his plans to the general welfare of the world, as can be learned from many facts, he neither incited Luther nor applauded him. Often he expressed his incessant, perpetual grief, as he feared greater conflicts. As a wise man, however, he did not only follow profane judgments, which order that the tender beginnings of all changes should be put down very quickly, but he also took God's norm into account. God's norm orders that the Gospel be heard and forbids opposition to the acknowledged truth and calls the stubbornness that opposes the truth a blasphemy condemned by God in horrible fashion. As a wise man, he did what many other godly and wise men have done: he yielded to God. He zealously read what was written, and what he judged to be true he had no wish to destroy. I also know that he often sought the opinions of learned and wise men on these very matters and that in the Imperial Diet (1520), which Emperor Charles the Fifth held after his coronation in the city of Cologne, he requested Erasmus of Rotterdam in a friendly manner to state openly whether in his judgment Luther was in error in these controversies concerning which he had especially delivered discourses. There Erasmus stated openly that Luther was correct in his thinking but that he missed mildness in him. On this matter Duke Frederick later on wrote to Luther in very serious strain and strongly exhorted him to moderate the roughness of his style. It is also known that Luther promised Cardinal Cajetan to be silent if silence were also imposed on his adversaries. From this it can be clearly perceived that at this time, to be sure, he had not yet determined to stir up other conflicts in turn but that he was eager for peace. But gradually he was dragged into other subjects of discussion because ignorant writers had assailed him on all sides.

163

Then there followed the disputations concerning divine and human laws and on the shameful profanation of the Lord's Supper and on the selling and applying of it for others. Here it became necessary to explain the whole doctrine of sacrifice and to demonstrate the use of the sacraments. When godly men now heard that idolatries in the monasteries should be avoided, they began to abandon the impious servitude. Accordingly Luther gave his interpretations of the doctrine of repentance, of the remission of sins, of faith, and of indulgences. To these he added next the distinction between divine and human laws, the doctrine on the use of the Lord's Supper and of other sacraments, and the doctrine on vows. And these were the points that were especially in conflict. The only reason that Eck had for raising the question of the power of the bishop of Rome was to inflame the hatred of the papists and rulers against him. But he retained the Apostolic, Nicene, and Athanasian Creeds in all their purity. Then in many writings he explained in fairly extensive detail what should be changed in human rites and traditions and the reason for this. And what he wanted to be retained and what form of doctrine and administration of the sacraments he accepted is clear from the confession which the duke of Saxony, Elector John, and Prince Philip, the Landgrave of Hess, delivered to Emperor Charles V at the Imperial Diet of Augs- 164 burg in 1530. The same is clear from the rites of the church in this city and from the doctrine which our church proclaims, the summary of which is clearly contained in the confession. I relate this that godly men may not only consider what errors Luther censured, and what idolatries he removed, but that they should also know that he embraced the whole doctrine of the church as necessary and restored purity in rites and demonstrated to godly men examples for the renewal of churches. And it is useful for posterity to know what Luther approved.[43]

II

The Ninety-five Theses and "A Sermon on Indulgence and Grace"

The Ninety-five Theses, 1517

Out of love and zeal for truth and the desire to bring it to light, the following theses will be publicly discussed at Wittenberg under the chairmanship of the reverend father Martin Luther, Master of Arts and Sacred Theology and regularly appointed Lecturer on these subjects at that place. He requests that those who cannot be present to debate orally with us will do so by letter.

WA 1:233

LW 31:25

In the Name of Our Lord Jesus Christ. Amen.[44]

1. When our Lord and Master Jesus Christ said, "Repent" [Matt. 4:17], he willed the entire life of believers to be one of repentance.

2. This word cannot be understood as referring to the sacrament of penance, that is, confession and satisfaction, as administered by the clergy.

3. Yet it does not mean solely inner repentance; such inner repentance is worthless unless it produces various outward mortifications of the flesh.

4. The penalty of sin remains as long as the hatred of self, that is, true inner repentance, until our entrance into the kingdom of heaven.

26

5. The pope neither desires nor is able to remit any penalties except those imposed by his own authority or that of the canons.

6. The pope cannot remit any guilt, except by declaring and showing that it has been remitted by God; or, to be sure, by remitting guilt in cases reserved to his judgment. If his right to grant remission in these cases were disregarded, the guilt would certainly remain unforgiven.

7. God remits guilt to no one unless at the same time he humbles him in all things and makes him submissive to his vicar, the priest.

8. The penitential canons are imposed only on the living, and, according to the canons themselves, nothing should be imposed on the dying.

9. Therefore the Holy Spirit through the pope is kind to us insofar as the pope in his decrees always makes exception of the article of death and of necessity.

10. Those priests act ignorantly and wickedly who, in the case of the dying, reserve canonical penalties for purgatory.

11. Those tares of changing the canonical penalty to the penalty of purgatory were evidently sown while the bishops slept [Matt. 13:25].

12. In former times canonical penalties were imposed, not after, but before absolution, as tests of true contrition.

234 13. The dying are freed by death from all penalties, are already dead as far as the canon laws are concerned, and have a right to be released from them.

14. Imperfect piety or love on the part of the dying person necessarily brings with it great fear; and the smaller the love, the greater the fear.

27 15. This fear or horror is sufficient in itself, to say nothing of other things, to constitute the penalty of purgatory, since it is very near the horror of despair.

16. Hell, purgatory, and heaven seem to differ the same as despair, fear, and assurance of salvation.

17. It seems as though for the souls in purgatory fear should necessarily decrease and love increase.

18. Furthermore, it does not seem proved, either by reason or Scripture, that souls in purgatory are outside the state of merit, that is, unable to grow in love.

19. Nor does it seem proved that souls in purgatory, at least not all of them, are certain and assured of their own salvation, even if we ourselves may be entirely certain of it.

20. Therefore the pope, when he uses the words "plenary remission of all penalties," does not actually mean "all penalties," but only those imposed by himself.

21. Thus those indulgence preachers are in error who say that a man is absolved from every penalty and saved by papal indulgences.

22. As a matter of fact, the pope remits to souls in purgatory no penalty which, according to canon law, they should have paid in this life.

23. If remission of all penalties whatsoever could be granted to anyone at all, certainly it would be granted only to the most perfect, that is, to very few.

24. For this reason most people are necessarily deceived by that indiscriminate and high-sounding promise of release from penalty.

25. That power which the pope has in general over purgatory corresponds to the power which any bishop or curate has in a particular way in his own diocese or parish.

26. The pope does very well when he grants remission to souls in purgatory, not by the power of the keys, which he does not have, but by way of intercession for them.

27. They preach only human doctrines who say that as soon as the money clinks into the money chest, the soul flies out of purgatory. 28

28. It is certain that when money clinks in the money chest, greed and avarice can be increased; but when the church intercedes, the result is in the hands of God alone.

29. Who knows whether all souls in purgatory wish to be redeemed, since we have exceptions in St. Severinus and St. Paschal, as related in a legend.

30. No one is sure of the integrity of his own contrition, much less of having received plenary remission.

31. The man who actually buys indulgences is as rare as he who is really penitent; indeed, he is exceedingly rare.

32. Those who believe that they can be certain of their salvation because they have indulgence letters will be eternally damned, together with their teachers.

235 33. Men must especially be on their guard against those who say that the pope's pardons are that inestimable gift of God by which man is reconciled to him.

34. For the graces of indulgences are concerned only with the penalties of sacramental satisfaction established by man.

35. They who teach that contrition is not necessary on the part of those who intend to buy souls out of purgatory or to buy confessional privileges preach unchristian doctrine.

36. Any truly repentant Christian has a right to full remission of penalty and guilt, even without indulgence letters.

29 37. Any true Christian, whether living or dead, participates in all the blessings of Christ and the church; and this is granted him by God, even without indulgence letters.

38. Nevertheless, papal remission and blessing are by no means to be disregarded, for they are, as I have said [Thesis 6], the proclamation of the divine remission.

39. It is very difficult, even for the most learned theologians, at one and the same time to commend to the people the bounty of indulgences and the need of true contrition.

40. A Christian who is truly contrite seeks and loves to pay penalties for his sins; the bounty of indulgences, however, relaxes penalties and causes men to hate them—at least it furnishes occasion for hating them.

41. Papal indulgences must be preached with caution, lest people erroneously think that they are preferable to other good works of love.

42. Christians are to be taught that the pope does not intend that the buying of indulgences should in any way be compared with works of mercy.

43. Christians are to be taught that he who gives to the poor or lends

to the needy does a better deed than he who buys indulgences.

44. Because love grows by works of love, man thereby becomes better. Man does not, however, become better by means of indulgences but is merely freed from penalties.

45. Christians are to be taught that he who sees a needy man and passes him by, yet gives his money for indulgences, does not buy papal indulgences but God's wrath.

46. Christians are to be taught that, unless they have more than they need, they must reserve enough for their family needs and by no means squander it on indulgences.

47. Christians are to be taught that the buying of indulgences is a matter of free choice, not commanded.

48. Christians are to be taught that the pope, in granting indulgences, needs and thus desires their devout prayer more than their money.

49. Christians are to be taught that papal indulgences are useful only if they do not put their trust in them, but very harmful if they lose 30 their fear of God because of them.

50. Christians are to be taught that if the pope knew the exactions of the indulgence preachers, he would rather that the basilica of St. Peter were burned to ashes than built up with the skin, flesh, and bones of his sheep.

51. Christians are to be taught that the pope would and should wish to give of his own money, even though he had to sell the basilica of St. Peter, to many of those from whom certain hawkers of indulgences cajole money.

52. It is vain to trust in salvation by indulgence letters, even though 236 the indulgence commissary, or even the pope, were to offer his soul as security.

53. They are enemies of Christ and the pope who forbid altogether the preaching of the Word of God in some churches in order that indulgences may be preached in others.

54. Injury is done the Word of God when, in the same sermon, an equal or larger amount of time is devoted to indulgences than to the Word.

55. It is certainly the pope's sentiment that if indulgences, which are a very insignificant thing, are celebrated with one bell, one procession, and one ceremony, then the gospel, which is the very greatest thing, should be preached with a hundred bells, a hundred processions, a hundred ceremonies.

56. The treasures of the church, out of which the pope distributes indulgences, are not sufficiently discussed or known among the people of Christ.

57. That indulgences are not temporal treasures is certainly clear, for many [indulgence] preachers do not distribute them freely but only gather them.

58. Nor are they the merits of Christ and the saints, for, even without the pope, the latter always work grace for the inner man, and the cross, death, and hell for the outer man.

59. St. Laurence said that the poor of the church were the treasures of the church, but he spoke according to the usage of the word in his own time.

60. Without want of consideration we say that the keys of the church, given by the merits of Christ, are that treasure;

61. For it is clear that the pope's power is of itself sufficient for the remission of penalities and cases reserved by himself.

62. The true treasure of the church is the most holy gospel of the glory and grace of God.

63. But this treasure is naturally most odious, for it makes the first to be last [Matt. 20:16].

64. On the other hand, the treasure of indulgences is naturally most acceptable, for it makes the last to be first.

65. Therefore the treasures of the gospel are nets with which one formerly fished for men of wealth.

66. The treasures of indulgences are nets with which one now fishes for the wealth of men.

67. The indulgences which the demagogues acclaim as the greatest graces are actually understood to be such only insofar as they promote gain.

68. They are nevertheless in truth the most insignificant graces when

31

compared with the grace of God and the piety of the cross.

69. Bishops and curates are bound to admit the commissaries of papal indulgences with all reverence.

70. But they are much more bound to strain their eyes and ears lest these men preach their own dreams instead of what the pope has commissioned.

71. Let him who speaks against the truth concerning papal indulgences be anathema and accursed;

72. But let him who guards against the lust and license of the indulgence preachers be blessed; 237

73. Just as the pope justly thunders against those who by any means whatsoever contrive harm to the sale of indulgences.

74. But much more does he intend to thunder against those who use indulgences as a pretext to contrive harm to holy love and truth. 32

75. To consider papal indulgences so great that they could absolve a man even if he had done the impossible and had violated the mother of God is madness.

76. We say on the contrary that papal indulgences cannot remove the very least of venial sins as far as guilt is concerned.

77. To say that even St. Peter, if he were now pope, could not grant greater graces is blasphemy against St. Peter and the pope.

78. We say on the contrary that even the present pope, or any pope whatsoever, has greater graces at his disposal, that is, the gospel, spiritual powers, gifts of healing, etc., as it is written in I Cor. 12[:28].

79. To say that the cross emblazoned with the papal coat of arms, and set up by the indulgence preachers, is equal in worth to the cross of Christ is blasphemy.

80. The bishops, curates, and theologians who permit such talk to be spread among the people will have to answer for this.

81. This unbridled preaching of indulgences makes it difficult even for learned men to rescue the reverence which is due the pope from slander or from the shrewd questions of the laity,

82. Such as: "Why does not the pope empty purgatory for the sake of holy love and the dire need of the souls that are there if he

redeems an infinite number of souls for the sake of miserable money with which to build a church? The former reasons would be most just; the latter is most trivial."

83. Again, "Why are funeral and anniversary masses for the dead continued and why does he not return or permit the withdrawal of the endowments founded for them, since it is wrong to pray for the redeemed?"

84. Again, "What is this new piety of God and the pope that for a consideration of money they permit a man who is impious and their enemy to buy out of purgatory the pious soul of a friend of God and do not rather, because of the need of that pious and beloved soul, free it for pure love's sake?"

85. Again, "Why are the penitential canons, long since abrogated and dead in actual fact and through disuse, now satisfied by the granting of indulgences as though they were still alive and in force?"

86. Again, "Why does not the pope, whose wealth is today greater than the wealth of the richest Crassus,[45] build this one basilica of St. Peter with his own money rather than with the money of poor believers?"

87. Again, "What does the pope remit or grant to those who by perfect contrition already have a right to full remission and blessings?"

88. Again, "What greater blessing could come to the church than if the pope were to bestow these remissions and blessings on every believer a hundred times a day, as he now does but once?"

89. "Since the pope seeks the salvation of souls rather than money by his indulgences, why does he suspend the indulgences and pardons previously granted when they have equal efficacy?"

90. To repress these very sharp arguments of the laity by force alone, and not to resolve them by giving reasons, is to expose the church and the pope to the ridicule of their enemies and to make Christians unhappy.

91. If, therefore, indulgences were preached according to the spirit and intention of the pope, all these doubts would be readily resolved. Indeed, they would not exist.

33

238

92. Away then with all those prophets who say to the people of Christ, "Peace, peace," and there is no peace! [Jer. 6:14].

93. Blessed be all those prophets who say to the people of Christ, "Cross, cross," and there is no cross!

94. Christians should be exhorted to be diligent in following Christ, their head, through penalties, death, and hell;

95. And thus be confident of entering into heaven through many tribulations rather than through the false security of peace [Acts 14:22].[46]

"A Sermon on Indulgence and Grace, 1518"

First. You should know that certain modern teachers such as the Master of the *Sentences* [Peter Lombard], St. Thomas, and their followers consider repentance to have three parts: contrition, confession, and satisfaction. Although this differentiation in keeping with their opinion is found to be hardly or not at all based on Holy Scripture or on the ancient holy Christian teachers, we want to let that stand for now and speak in their manner. WA 1:243

Second. They say indulgence removes not the first or second parts (that is, contrition or confession) but the third part (that is, satisfaction).

Third. Satisfaction is further divided into three parts: praying, fasting, almsgiving. Praying consists in all kinds of work that pertains to the soul: reading, meditating, hearing God's Word, preaching, teaching, and the like. Fasting consists in all kinds of work for the reproving of one's flesh, as being watchful, working, a hard bed, appropriate clothing, and so on. Almsgiving consists in all kinds of good work of love and mercy to one's neighbors. 244

Fourth. All of them have no doubt that indulgence removes the works of satisfaction that are due or imposed because of sins; for if indulgence were to remove all of these works, no good works would remain for us to do.

Fifth. For many people there has been an important and as yet indecisive question whether indulgence also removes something more than such prescribed good works, that is, whether indulgence also removes the suffering that God's righteousness demands for sins.

Sixth. I let that question stand unchallenged for the moment. Let me state that it cannot be proved from Scripture that God's righteousness requires or demands some suffering or satisfaction from the sinner other than his sincere and genuine contrition or reform, with the resolution to carry Christ's cross from then on and to perform the aforementioned works (even if no one prescribes them). For He says through Ezekiel: Whenever a sinner repents and does right, I will no longer remember his sin [Ezek. 18:21; 33:14–16]. So He absolved even all these: Mary Magdalene, the palsied man, the adultress, and so on. And I should be delighted to hear anyone prove something else, even though certain scholars thought so.

Seventh. We find it is true that God punishes some according to His righteousness or that through suffering He draws them to contrition, as in Psalm 88 [89:31–34]: If his children sin, I will visit their sins with the rod; but My mercy I will yet not turn away from them. Remission of this suffering is in no man's power, but only in God's. He will not remit it but promises that He will impose it.

Eighth. Therefore no one can give a name to this so-called suffering; and no one knows what it is if it is not this punishment, also not the aforementioned good works.

Ninth. I say: Even if the Christian church right now would decide and declare that indulgence removes more than the works of satisfaction, it would still be a thousand times better if no Christian man would buy or desire indulgence but if they would rather do the works and bear the suffering. For indulgence is nothing else—cannot be anything else—than a release from good works and wholesome suffering which men should rather welcome than avoid (despite the fact that some modern preachers have invented two kinds of suffering: remedial and satisfactory, that is, some suffering from satisfaction and some for improvement). But we have more freedom to despise (God be praised!) the likes of such prattle than they have to invent it. For all suffering—yes, everything God imposes—is beneficial and useful to Christians.

Tenth. There is no point in arguing that the suffering and work are too much for a man to be able to carry out in his short lifetime and that he, therefore, needs indulgence. I replay that that has no basis in fact and is sheer invention. For God and the holy church impose no more on man than he can bear. St. Paul also says so: God does not allow anyone to be tempted more than he can bear [1 Cor. 10:13]. And it is no small disgrace for Christianity that it is charged with imposing more than we can bear.

Eleventh. Even if acts of penance as established in canon law were still in effect, stating that for every deadly sin seven years of penance were imposed, Christianity would still have to let them be established without imposing more than a person can bear. Since they are now not in effect, all the more care should be exercised not to impose more than a man can readily bear.

Twelfth. People actually say that with the rest of the suffering the sinner should be directed either into purgatory or to indulgences. But there are obviously more things said without basis in fact and without proof!

Thirteenth. It is a grievous error for anyone to think that he can make satisfaction for his own sins. God always forgives them out of His priceless grace and demands nothing more than a good life thereafter. Christianity actually does demand something. Therefore, it can and also should remit it and impose nothing severe or unbearable.

Fourteenth. Indulgence is allowed for the sake of imperfect and lazy Christians who refuse to be bold in good works or are unbearable. For indulgence helps no one improve but tolerates people's imperfection. Therefore, no one should speak against indulgence, but also no one should be persuaded in their direction.

Fifteenth. A man is much more safe and better off if he gives a stipulated amount for the building of St. Peter's or any other project simply for God's sake than if he buys indulgence for it. It is dangerous to give something for indulgence's sake and not for God's sake.

Sixteenth. It is much better to benefit someone in need with a good work than to give to a building. It is also much better than buying indulgence for that purpose. As I said before, it is better to do one good work than to be excused from many. But indulgence releases from many good works, or there is no release at all.

So that I may instruct you properly, mark this well: you should above all (without regard either for St. Peter's Church or indulgence) 246 give to your poor neighbor if you want to give anything. But if it should so happen that there are no more people in your city who need help (that will never happen, as God wills), then you should give as you wish to the churches, altars, adornment, and chalice in your city. And if there is also no more need of that, then you can give, if you wish, to St. Peter's Church or somewhere else. Even then you should not give for indulgence's sake, for St. Paul says: Whoever does not take care of his fellows is no Christian and worse than a pagan [1 Tim. 5:8]. Keep this in mind: whoever tells you something else is either misleading you or really seeking your soul in your purse. If he should find a penny there, it would please him more than all souls.

So you say: Then I shall never buy indulgence anymore. I reply: I have already said above that my desire, longing, request, and advice is that no one buy indulgence; let the lazy, sleepy Christians buy indulgence; tend to your own affairs.

Seventeenth. Indulgence is not commanded, not advised. It is counted among those things that are permitted and allowed. Therefore, it is not a work of obedience, not a matter of merit, but an excuse from obedience. Therefore, while people should prevent no one from buying the same, still people should draw Christians away from it and stimulate and strengthen them for the good works and suffering that are remitted by indulgence.

Eighteenth. Whether souls are drawn out of purgatory through indulgence, I do not know. Still I do not believe it, even though some modern scholars say so. But they cannot prove it, and the church has not established it yet. Therefore, to be more certain, it is much better that you pray for them yourself and do your work. This is better proved and is certain.

Nineteenth. In these points I do not have doubts, and they are sufficiently based on Scripture. Therefore, you should also have no doubts about them and let the Scholastic scholars be scholastic. They are not sufficient, the whole lot of them with their opinions, to substantiate a single sermon.

Twentieth. Even though some are now probably calling me a heretic—this truth is very detrimental to their treasury—I do not pay much attention to their bawling, for their reactions are those of clouded minds that never got a sniff of Scripture, never read the Christian teachers, never understood their own teachers, but are almost decayed in their riddled and mangled opinions. If they had understood these, they would know they ought to defame no man unheard and unchallenged. But may God give them and us right understanding. Amen.[47]

III

The Letters of Luther in Connection
with the Ninety-five Theses

TO ALBERT OF MAINZ, 31 OCTOBER 1517[48]

Most Reverend Father in Christ, Most Illustrious Sovereign: WABr 1:110

Forgive me that I, the least of all men, have the temerity to consider writing to Your Highness. The Lord Jesus is my witness that I LW 48:45 have long hesitated doing this on account of my insignificance and unworthiness, of which I am well aware. I do it now impudently, and 46 I am motivated solely by the obligation of my loyalty, which I know I owe you, Most Reverend Father in Christ. May Your Highness there- 111 fore deign to glance at what is but a grain of dust and, for the sake of your episcopal kindness, listen to my request.[49]

Under your most distinguished name, papal indulgences are offered all across the land for the construction of St. Peter. Now, I do not so much complain about the quacking of the preachers, which I haven't heard; but I bewail the gross misunderstanding among the people which comes from these preachers and which they spread everywhere among common men. Evidently the poor souls believe that when they have bought indulgence letters they are then assured of their salvation. They are likewise convinced that souls escape from purgatory as soon as they have placed a contribution into the chest.

69

Further, they assume that the grace obtained through these indulgences is so completely effective that there is no sin of such magnitude that it cannot be forgiven—even if (as they say) someone should rape the Mother of God, were this possible. Finally they also believe that man is freed from every penalty and guilt by these indulgences.

O great God! The souls committed to your care, excellent Father, are thus directed to death. For all these souls you have the heaviest and a constantly increasing responsibility. Therefore I can no longer be silent on this subject. No man can be assured of his salvation by any episcopal function. He is not even assured of his salvation by the infusion of God's grace, because the Apostle [Paul] orders us to work out our salvation constantly "in fear and trembling" [Phil. 2:12]. Even 47 "the just will hardly be saved" [1 Pet. 4:18]. Finally the way that leads to life is so narrow that the Lord, through the prophets Amos and Zechariah, calls those that will be saved "a brand plucked out of the fire" [Amos 4:11; Zech. 3:2]. And everywhere else the Lord proclaims the difficulty of salvation. How can the [indulgence agents] then make the people feel secure and without fear [concerning salvation] by means of those false stories and promises of pardon? After all, the indulgences contribute absolutely nothing to the salvation and holiness of souls; they only compensate for the external punishment which—on the basis of Canon Law—once used to be imposed.

Works of piety and love are infinitely better than indulgences; and yet [the indulgence preachers] do not preach them with an equally big display and effort. What is even worse, [the preachers] are silent about them because they have to preach the sale of the indulgences. The first and only duty of the bishops, however, is to see that the people learn the gospel and the love of Christ. For on no occasion has Christ ordered that indulgences should be preached, but he forcefully commanded the gospel to be preached. What a horror, what a danger for a bishop to permit the loud noise of indulgences among his people, while the gospel is silenced, and to be more concerned with the sale of indulgences than with the gospel! Will not Christ say to [such bishops], "You strain out a gnat but swallow a camel" [Matt. 23:24]?

Added to all this, my Most Reverend Father in the Lord, is the fact that in the *Instruction* for the indulgence agents which is published

under Your Highness' name, it is written (certainly without your full
awareness and consent, Most Reverend Father) that one of the prin- 112
cipal graces [bestowed through the indulgences] is that inestimable
gift of God by which man is reconciled with God and by which all the
punishments of purgatory are blotted out. It is also written there that 48
contrition is not necessary on the part of those who buy off their
souls or acquire *confessionalia*.

What can I do, excellent Bishop and Most Illustrious Sovereign? I
can only beg you, Most Reverend Father, through the Lord Jesus
Christ, to deign to give this matter your fatherly attention and totally
withdraw that little book and command the preachers of indulgences
to preach in another way. If this is not done, someone may rise and, by
means of publications, silence those preachers and refute the little
book. This would be the greatest disgrace for Your Most Illustrious
Highness. I certainly shudder at this possibility, yet I am afraid it will
happen if things are not quickly remedied.

I beg Your Most Illustrious Grace to accept this faithful service of
my humble self in a princely and episcopal—that is, in the most
kind—way, just as I am rendering it with a most honest heart, and in
absolute loyalty to you, Most Reverend Father. For I, too, am a part of
your flock. May the Lord Jesus protect you, Most Reverend Father, forever. Amen.

From Wittenberg, October 31, 1517.

Were it agreeable to you, Most Reverend Father, you could examine my disputation theses, so that you may see how dubious is this 49
belief concerning indulgences, which these preachers propagate as if it
were the surest thing in the whole world.[50]

Your unworthy son, Martin Luther, Augustinian, called Doctor
of Sacred Theology.[51]

To George Spalatin,[52] First Days
of November 1517[53]

Greetings! I had determined, dear Spalatin, never to communicate WABr 1:118
the *Dialog*[54] to anyone. My only reason is that it has been composed so
pleasantly, so learnedly, and in short, so ingeniously, that is, in a manner so altogether Erasmian, that it makes one laugh and joke at the

faults and miseries of the church of Christ, which should nevertheless form the subject of complaint to God on the part of every Christian with the deepest sighs. But because you ask for it, here you have it! Read it and make use of it and then return it.

I did not want my theses to fall into the hands of our illustrious prince or anyone from his court before those who have seen them who believe they are branded in them,[55] so that they do not come to believe that they were published by me either by the orders or favor of the prince against the bishop of Magdeburg.[56] This, as I hear, is already being dreamed by many of them. But it is now safe to swear that they were published without the knowledge of Duke Frederick. Another time more! I am having a very busy time. Farewell! From our monastery.

Brother Martin Eleutherius,[57] Augustinian of Wittenberg.

You wrote me that a gown has been promised me by the prince. I would like to know to whom he gave the commission about this matter.[58]

To John Lang, 11 November 1517[59]

WABr 1:121   My Reverend Father in Christ, I am sending you another new[60] paradox. But if your theologians also take offense at these and say, as all men are saying everywhere about me, that I am all too rash and proud in passing judgment and in condemning the opinions of others, my reply through you and by this letter is as follows. First, their mature moderation and long-suffering sobriety would be highly pleasing to me if they were to exhibit it in practice as they find fault with me for levity and headlong rashness. For I see they do not find it hard to note such a fault in me.[61]

But I am surprised that they do not look at their Aristotle with the same eyes, or if they look at him, that they do not see that Aristotle is nothing else in almost every sentence and clause than a faultfinder and indeed a faultfinder of faultfinders. Accordingly, if that heathen is still accepted, read, and cited without the fault of biting rashness proving an obstacle, why is it that I, a Christian, am so unacceptable, especially since in some respects I have a flavor similar to this most acceptable Aristotle? Or is a drop of the fault displeasing in me when a whole sea of it gives pleasure in Aristotle?

I am also surprised that they do not hate and condemn themselves in similar fashion. For what are these Scholastics toward one another but pure critics, people like Aristarchus, mutual faultfinders? They are permitted and are welcome to judge the opinions of all, but the same thing is completely forbidden to me. Finally, I also make this complaint: if my opinion is so utterly displeasing to them and they prefer to praise moderation, why do they not also restrain themselves from passing judgment on me? Why do they not wait for the outcome of the matter with more moderation? So you see how we are human, that is, quite unjust; how we are always in a hurry to pluck motes from the eyes of brethren and in the meantime find delight in the beams in our own eyes, also as far as this life is concerned. Again, someone else's fault we strain out like a gnat; in us it is a camel, and yet we swallow it as if it were the highest virtue.

Accordingly you see that I do not regard those ghosts of the faultfinders as more than the ghosts they actually are, and I refuse to be disturbed by their approval or disapproval. On the question of my rashness or moderation I know for sure that if I am moderate, the truth will not grow more noble by my moderation; and if I am rash, it will not grow more ignoble by my rashness. The one wish that I would like to have fulfilled by you and your theologians with all my heart is this: they should for the time being keep quiet about the faults of the author and let me know what they think about my publications or conclusions themselves, or rather, that they indicate to me the faults of error, if there are any in them. For who does not know that nothing new can be brought forth without pride or at least without the appearance of pride and suspicion of contention? For even granted that humility itself is attempting something new, it will immediately be brought under the fault of pride by those who are of another view. For why were Christ and all the martyrs put to death? Why have teachers suffered envy? Only because they seemed to be proud and despisers of the old renowned wisdom and prudence or because they brought forth such new matters without the advice of those who held the old views.

I do not want them to expect from me that humility, that is, hypocrisy, that they should believe that I should make use of their advice and decision before I go into publication.[62] For I do not want

122

what I am doing to be put into effect by the activity or advice of men, but of God. For if it is a work of God, who will hinder it? If it is not of God, who will promote it? Let not my will, nor theirs, nor ours, but Thine be done, Holy Father, who art in heaven! Amen.

To Jerome Schulz, Bishop of Brandenburg, 13 February 1518[63]

WABr 1:138 When new and unprecedented doctrines on papal indulgences began to be heard recently in our precincts, excellent Bishop, so that very many learned as well as unlearned men were surprised and disturbed on all sides, I was requested in many conversations and letters coming to me from both friends and those personally unknown to me to give my views on the novelty, not to say, presumption of these words. For a time I pretended not to be concerned, but finally they pressed their argument with sharp disputations even to the point of imperiling the regard for the pope. What was I to do? It was not my business to determine anything in this matter, and I was afraid to contradict those who I wished with all my heart would seem to have preached nothing but the truth. But these men were so insistent with clear arguments in proving the falsity and inanity [of these dogmas] that, to confess the truth, they completely convinced and captivated me.[64] Therefore, that I might satisfy both groups, it seemed the best plan neither to agree nor to disagree with either party, but for the time being to hold discussion on such an important matter[65] until the holy church might determine what opinion was to be held. Accordingly, I announced a disputation,[66] inviting and requesting all men publicly, but as you know, all the most learned men privately, to make known their opinion in writing.[67] For I saw that in these matters neither the Scriptures nor the teachers of the church nor the canons themselves (with the exception of a few canonists who spoke without a text and some of the Scholastic teachers who thought likewise but also offered no proof) were against me.[68]

—⁂—

139 Therefore, when I summoned all into the arena but no one came forward and I saw that my theses had spread more widely

than I wished and that they were received everywhere not as something for discussion but as assertions,[69] I was compelled contrary to my wishes and desires to bring my want of eloquence and ignorance out into the public and to publish before the people the statements and proofs of them, thinking that I would be doing the wiser thing if I incurred the infamy of being inexperienced rather than that I should allow those to err who happen to think that all has been asserted. Among these matters are some that I doubt, some that I do not know, some that I deny, but none that I assert obstinately. Moreover, I submit all matters to the holy church and its judgments.

... Accordingly, most clement Bishop, may you regard it worthy to take up these trifles of mine, and that all men may know that I am not making any bold assertion, I not only permit you, but even beg you, as my honored father, to take up your pen and to strike out whatever you please or to make a fire and to burn up the whole thing! It makes no difference to me at all! I know that Christ does 140 not need me and that without me He will proclaim what is good for His church. If it is not His work, I do not want it in any way to be my work, but that it should be nothing and no one's work. And since, according to Gregory of Nazianzus, it is not safe to speak the truth in the church, especially to grave sinners, I have not forgotten who I am, and I testify that with these words I am disputing and not finally settling the issue. I am disputing, I say, not making assertions; and I am disputing with fear. Not that I fear the bulls and threats of those who are not at all touched by any fear and want to believe as gospel whatever they have dreamed. For the boldness and ignorance of these men, I admit it, has at the same time compelled me not to yield to my fear. If this [boldness] were not so great, no one outside of my corner would have known me. I was not obliged to seek anything except that I should not be an occasion of error to anyone. Let Him alone receive honor to whom it belongs and who is blessed forever! Amen. May He preserve you for us and long and prosperously direct you, excellent Bishop. I hope you are well and I ask that you wish me well.

To Christoph Scheurl,[70] 5 March 1518

WABr 1:151 I have received two letters from you, my excellent and learned friend Christoph, one in Latin and the other in the vernacular. At the same 152 time also [there arrived] the gift of that excellent gentleman Albrecht Dürer,[71] as well as my theses in Latin and German.[72] In regard to the first point on which you express surprise—that I did not send them to you—my reply is that it was not my plan or desire to bring them out among the people, but to exchange views on them with a few men who lived in our neighborhood so that on the judgment of many they might either be condemned and rejected or approved and published.[73] But now, far beyond my expectation, they are printed so often[74] and distributed that this production is causing me regrets; not that I am not in favor of the truth becoming known to the people— no! rather it is my one and only quest—but this method is not a suitable one to instruct the people. For some matters are doubtful to me myself, and I would have asserted or omitted some matters far differently and with more certainty if I had hoped that this would ensue. However, I understand fairly well from this dissemination what the opinion on indulgences is among all men everywhere, even though it is kept secret, evidently "because of a fear of the Jews." And so I was forced to prepare proofs[75] for them; but permission has not yet been given to publish them because my worthy and gracious Lord Bishop of Brandenburg, whose judgment I consulted in this matter, has been very busy and is delaying me for a long time.[76] To be sure, if the Lord grants me leisure, I want to publish a pamphlet in German on the power of indulgences,[77] in order to attack those very vague theses. As far as I can see, there is no doubt that the people are being deceived, not by indulgences, but by their use. Therefore I shall send them [the *Resolutions*] as soon as they have been completed.

In the meantime I request you to commend me to that excellent gentleman, Albrecht Dürer, and tell him that I am thankful to him and have him in my thoughts. But I ask you and him that you set aside your very unfair opinion of me and do not expect more of me than I can perform. I can do nothing and am nothing at all, and I am becoming more of a nothing daily.

To Jodocus Trutfetter,[78] 9 May 1518

Concerning the other theses on indulgences, however, I wrote to you previously[79] that I was not pleased with their wide dissemination. What is happening is unheard of, and I have no reason to hope that what happened in their case alone would come to pass. Otherwise I would have set them up more clearly, as I did in the "Sermon" in the vernacular,[80] which displeases you more than all of these matters. WABr 1:170

I ask you, my lord and my father in the Lord, does it not also displease you that Christ's wretched people are being harassed and mocked for so long by indulgences? Is the remission of temporal and arbitrary satisfaction such a great matter that the people must jeopardize their faith? There is hardly a man who does not believe that he obtains something of as great value as the grace of God by means of indulgences. It was a good thing that we first uncovered the matter lest, while we draw a veil over it, men eventually of themselves come to understand those pious deceptions—as men call them—of venal mongers, most impious tricks in actual fact, and pay us back as we have deserved. For my part, I acknowledge that I would prefer to have no indulgences in the whole church. The Italians also are not a whit concerned about them except to increase filthy lucre to such an extent. To be sure, they increase filthy lucre and nothing else, as I state more extensively in my *Proofs* which are to be published, God willing, immediately.

I am surprised, however, that you could actually bring yourself to believe that I was the instigator of the burning of Tetzel's theses.[81] Do you believe that all human feelings have perished in me to such an extent that I, a monk and a theologian, would have inflicted such a striking injustice in a matter that did not concern me on a man of such high rank? But what am I to do when all men believe everyone about everything concerning me? Am I able to check and anticipate the tongues of all men? Let them say, hear, and believe, whoever they may be, whatever it is that they have a liking for, and wherever they want to do so. I shall do whatever the Lord grants, and I shall have no fears nor ever become presumptuous, if God grants it. 171

TO POPE LEO X,[82] MAY 1518

WA 1:527 To the Most Holy Father, Leo X, Pope,
Brother Martin Luther, Augustinian, Wishes Eternal Salvation.

I have heard the worst report about myself, Most Holy Father. From it I understand that certain friends have slandered me most seriously before you and your associates, alleging that I have endeavored to threaten the authority and power of the keys and of the Supreme Pontiff. I am called heretic, apostate, infidel, and am accused by six hundred names—no! by six hundred shames! My ears ring and my eyes fail. But the only steady support I can trust, my innocent and peaceful conscience, stands firm. I hear nothing new. For with such distinctions have I been decorated also in our area by those highly honorable, truthful men, that is, people with a very bad conscience, who try to unload their monstrosities on me and glorify their own shames with my shame. But, Most Holy Father, may you deign to hear the facts of the case from me, even though I am unrhetorical and unrefined.

That jubilee of the apostolic indulgences began to be preached among us recently. It got to the point that its preachers thought they were permitted to go to any lengths because of the fear of your name. They dared to proclaim the most wicked, heretical teachings leading to a most serious scandal and ridicule of ecclesiastical power. They 528 acted as if the decretals *De abusionibus quaestorum* ["On the Malpractice of Indulgence Preachers"] did not apply to them. They were not satisfied to spread their own poison about with their impudent sermons. They even published booklets and spread them among the people. I shall omit their insatiable, unprecedented greed which absolutely reeks in almost every single syllable. In their booklets they have set down these same wicked, heretical teachings, and they have done so in such a way that confessors are forced by oath to impart these same teachings to the people most faithfully and urgently. I speak the truth. There is no place where they can hide themselves from the heat of my accusation. Their booklets are available, and they cannot deny them. They were then carrying on a profitable business, and the people were being fleeced with false hopes. As the prophet says [Micah 3:2], they tore the skin off their bones; but they themselves were faring sumptuously and delightfully.

There was one way in which they checked scandal: the fear of your name, the intimidation of the stake, and the shame of the name heretic. It is really incredible how they were inclined to threaten, when they noted opposition even to their most trifling ideas and matters of pure opinion. Yet if this is the way to check scandal, it is all the more the way to give rise to sheer, tyrannical schism and sedition.

But nevertheless, rumors were spreading through the taverns about the greed of priests, and slander rose against the keys and the Supreme Pontiff—the common talk of this whole world is witness. Yet I was burning, as I confess, with the zeal for Christ as it seemed to me—or if you wish, with the fire of youth. Still I did not see that it was my duty to establish or do anything in these matters. For that reason I privately warned a few prelates of the church.[83] Here I was accepted by some and ridiculed by others; some saw me in one light and others in another. Actually the fear of your name and the intimidation of censure were predominant considerations. Finally, when I could do nothing else, I decided to give at least some little evidence against them, that is, to call their teachings into question and debate.[84] So I published a disputation list and invited only the more learned men to see if perhaps some might wish to debate with me. That must be clear even to my opponents on the basis of the introduction to that debate.

Behold, this is the fire with which, they complain, the whole world is ablaze. Perhaps they say so because they consider it improper that I alone—a teacher of theology by your apostolic authority—should have the right to hold disputation in public assembly according to the custom of all universities and of the whole church not only about indulgences but also about *divine* power, remission, indulgence—far more significant matters. I was not moved much by the fact that they were jealous of the status accorded me by the power of Your Holiness. Reluctantly I am forced to countenance much more serious acts on their part: they mix the dreams of Aristotle into the very heart of theology; they debate on the divine majesty in a trifling way contrary to and beyond the privilege accorded them.

Furthermore, it is a mystery to me that fate spread only these my theses beyond the others—not only my own but those of all teachers—so that they spread to almost the whole world. They were published only among our people and for our people's sake; and they

529 were published in such a way that I cannot believe everyone under-stood them. They are theses, after all, not teachings, not dogmas, phrased rather obscurely and paradoxically, as is the custom. Had I been able to foresee the results, I would have taken due precaution on my part to make them more easily understood.[85]

To Frederick the Wise, 21 (?) November[86] 1518

WABr 1:244 One thing causes me the deepest grief: that the Most Reverend Lord Legate is snapping at Your Most Illustrious Lordship with his letter as 245 though I were stirring up all these matters in dependence on the power of Your Highness. For certain sycophants also in our midst have spread the report that I have conducted these disputations on the exhortation and advice of Your Highness.[87] In actual fact, not even any of my intimate friends was aware of this disputation except the Most Reverend Lord Archbishop of Magdeburg and Lord Jerome, Bishop of Brandenburg. For as it was in their interest to prevent such mon-strous abuses, I humbly and reverently warned these men by private letters, before I should publish the disputation, that they should watch over Christ's sheep against these wolves. I well knew that these matters were to be referred not to the secular government but first to the bish-ops.[88] My letter is extant, after having passed through the hands of many men, as a witness of all these matters.[89] This is what I did.

To Nicholas Amsdorf, 1 November 1527

WABr 4:275 . . . in this way there are conflicts externally, fears inwardly, and those fairly severe. Christ is visiting us.[90] There is one consolation: we are opposing Satan in his madness, namely, that we at least have God's Word for the preservation of souls of believers, even though he may devour their bodies. Therefore, commend us to the brethren and to yourself that you may pray for us and that we may bravely endure the hand of the Lord and overcome Satan's might and guile, whether it be by death or by life. Amen. Written at Wittenberg on the day of All Saints, in the tenth year after the indulgences had been trampled underfoot,[91] in memory of which we are drinking at this hour,[92] com-forted in both directions. 1527.

IV

Luther's Words on the Theses in His Table Talk[93]

THE COLLECTION OF VEIT DIETRICH AND NICHOLAS MEDLER, FIRST HALF OF THE 1530S

884. In the year [15]16 I began to write against the papacy. In the year [15]18 Doctor Staupitz released me from obedience to my order and left me alone in Augsburg. In [15]19 Pope Leo excommunicated me from his church, and so I was released for a second time. In [15]21 Emperor Charles excommunicated me from the empire, and so I was released for the third time. But the Lord took me up, Psalm 25 [27:10]. In the year [15]19 I disputed at Leipzig with Eck on the Vigil of Peter and Paul.

WATr 1:441–42

885. Staupitz once said to me: "Master Martin, get yourself a doctor's degree, and you will have your work cut out for you." In the following year this prophecy was fulfilled; it then produced the questions concerning penance, indulgences, and other traditions of the pope.

WATr 1:442

The Collection of Cordatus,
18 August to 26 December 1531

WATr 2:376   2250. I, Martin Luther, was born in the year 1483. My father was called John and my mother Hannah. My fatherland was Mansfeld. My father died in 1530, and my mother, named Hannah, died in 1531.

In the year 1516 I began to write against the pope. In the year [15]18 Doctor Staupitz released me from obedience to my order and left me alone at Augsburg when I had been summoned before Emperor Maximilian and the pope's legate, who was then at the place. In the year [15]19 Pope Leo excommunicated me from the church, and so I was released for a second time. In the year [15]21 Emperor Charles excommunicated me from his empire, and so I was released a third time. But the Lord took me up.

WATr 2:379   2255a. When Staupitz, my prior, was once sitting in reflection under the pear tree that is still standing in the middle of my courtyard, he eventually said to me: "Sir Master, you must get yourself the doctor's degree, and you will have your work cut out for you." This also ensued in the second year after taking my doctorate, when I published the theses on penance and indulgences.

When he met me a second time under the pear tree concerning the same matter and I began to withstand him, bringing up many reasons and especially also that my strength was consumed so that a long life could not be left for me, Staupitz replied to these objections: "Do you not know that our Lord God has many matters of importance to carry out? For these He requires many clever and wise people to help Him with advice. When you come to die, you have to be His adviser." But at that time I did not understand that this prophecy would have to be fulfilled in this manner. For after four years I began to wage war against the pope and all that is his.

WATr 2:379   2255b. When Doctor Staupitz was once taking a walk and reflecting under the pear tree in the garden and saw Martin, he said: "Sir Master, become a doctor of theology, and you will have your work cut out for you." In the second year this prophecy was fulfilled, for Doctor Martin set in motion the questions about penance, indulgences, and the other traditions of the pope.

THE COLLECTION OF CORDATUS,
22 JANUARY TO 28 MARCH 1532

2455a. In the year [15]17 on the day of All Saints I began for the first WATr 2:467
time to write against the pope and indulgences. In the year [15]18 I
was excommunicated. In the year [15]19 I disputed at Leipzig with
Eck.

2455b. In the year 1517 on the Feast of All Saints I began for the first WATr 2:467
time to write against the papacy and indulgences. In the year 1518 I
was excommunicated. In [15]19 I disputed at Leipzig.

THE TRANSCRIPTS
OF ANTON LAUTERBACH AND JEROME WELLER,
1 NOVEMBER TO 21 DECEMBER 1537

3644c. The course of Doctor Luther's doctrine. "In the year 1505 I WATr 3:477
graduated with the title of master, and in that year I entered the
monastery. In [15]08 I came to Wittenberg. In [15]10 I traveled to
Rome. In [15]12 on the day of St. Lucy [Dec. 13] I was graduated as a
doctor of theology by Doctor Andrew Carlstadt. Soon afterwards I
lectured on the Psalter, the Epistle to the Hebrews, and then on
Romans and Titus. In [15]17 I began to write against Tetzel concerning penance and indulgences; I delivered lectures on the Ten Commandments and on the Psalms a second time. Eventually I experienced hindrances in regard to these. I had to come to blows with the
pope and the sophists. Then I was summoned to the Imperial Diet of
Worms. I was there for nearly two years. I wrote sermons and several
psalms. I also kept up the fight with the pope and then with the
Enthusiasts."

ANTON LAUTERBACH'S JOURNAL FOR 1538,
2 FEBRUARY 1538

3722. Now God has guided us in a wonderful manner and for more WATr 3:564
than 20 years has brought me into the contest. How difficult it was to
get things moving at the beginning when we were going to Kemberg
in the year 1517 on the day after All Saints. Here I had first deter-

mined to write against the crass errors of indulgences. Doctor Jerome Schurff opposed me. "Do you want to write against the pope?" he asked. "What do you want to do? They will not put up with it." I said, "And if they must put up with it?" Soon Sylvester, the master of the sacred palace, came into the arena fulminating against me with this syllogism: "Whoever has doubts about one word or deed of the Roman Church is a heretic; Luther has doubts about the word of the Roman Church and its method of actions; therefore, etc." Then things got started! [There are parallels in Aurifaber 22, 115; 58, 3; and Förstemann-Bindseil 2421; 4387.]

Anton Lauterbach's Journal for 1539, 25 and 29 March 1539

WATr 4:316 4446. At the beginning of the Gospel [that is, the Reformation] I proceeded gradually against Tetzel in his shamelessness, and Jerome, the bishop of Brandenburg, esteemed me highly. I also urged him as the WATr 4:317 *Ordinarius Loci* to have a look at this matter, and I sent him the *Resolutions* written in my hand before I published them. But no one wanted to curb Tetzel's barking, but men had the presumption to defend him. So I was foolish enough to come forward while others listened and became fatigued under tyranny. Now that I have entered the fray, may God continue His help to me! For one can never repay the pope what he has coming.

Table Talk from the Year 1540 (Attributed to Mathesius, but Apparently Not by Him), Summer 1540

WATr 5:74 5343. Concerning his theses. The Doctor said: "The papists had a bad conscience when at first I at least brought some matters into doubt, as my first theses set forth: 'Our Lord and Master,' etc. I have shocked all the ecclesiasticals. Cardinal Raphael sent a letter to Elector Frederick and praised him from his ancestors on and I know not what else. Later he added: 'And I hear that you have a monk who is highly gifted and wants to overthrow the authority of the church.' In short, he wanted the prince to burn me. But because he had a sharp intellect, he at once detected that the Romanists had a bad case.

"And Pfeffinger [a councilor of Frederick the Wise] came to Maximilian. He saw my theses and asked: 'What is your monk doing? His theses certainly do not merit contempt.' So a certain abbot came to the bishop of Brandenburg [Jerome Schulz] and exhorted him to calm these disturbances I had raised; but the bishop sent the abbot to me. He came to me and conferred with me, but it came to nothing. They were all afraid."

5346. The prior at Kemberg [Bartholomew Bernhardi] was my only disciple. He told me many things as to what the doctors and masters said, and he asked me to conduct a disputation. These disputations of the year [15]16 are still extant. WATr 5:76

About this same time Tetzel preached indulgences at Jüterbog, and people ran there like maniacs. I began gradually to dissuade men and to set forth what grace and remission of sins are. But when Tetzel proceeded with greater impudence, I disputed concerning indulgences. This matter stirred up the whole world. At this time I acknowledged the pope as my lord and thought that I would be dealing with a matter pleasing to him; but he attacked me with all his might. Therefore, I had to defend myself, and I have really defended myself until indulgences, monasteries, Mass, and foundations have tottered. And the pope will also soon follow them. In this way God has attacked the pope in all his strength with the greatest of weakness, and He will throw him down by weakness; let the devil rage and rave, etc.

Table Talk from the Year 1540 (Attributed to Mathesius, but Apparently Not by Him), 7 August 1540

5347. From an autograph of Sir Doctor. "I was born in 1484 at Mansfeld. This is certain! In 1497 [in the transcript corrected from 1494] I was sent to school at Magdeburg. I spent a year there. In 1501 I came from Eisenach to Erfurt. I was at Eisenach for four years. In 1505 at the beginning of the year I became a master. In 1505 at the end of the same year I became a monk. In 1508 I came to Wittenberg. In 1510 I WATr 5:76 WATr 5:77

was at Rome, where the devil has his seat. In 1517 I began to dispute about indulgences. In 1519 the Leipzig debate was held. I married in 1525. I was 56 in 1540. In 1518 I was at Augsburg, in 1521 at Worms, and in 1529 at Marburg."

WATr 5:77 5349. The account of the poverty and knighthood of Doctor Martin and the *Acta Augustana* in the presence of Cajetan. When Doctor Martin saw pigs in his yard, he said: "Here there was a holy temple; in this church [the older monastery church demolished later because of its dilapidated condition] I first preached."

At that time Tetzel brought indulgences to Jüterbog, for the prince refused to admit him. The people used to flock together to hear Tetzel there and bring home what they had heard in Jüterbog: "If anyone had violated the Virgin Mary, my indulgences would be of service to him," and "I carry about with me more power than Peter and Paul had." Moved by these impious statements, the Doctor began to dissuade people from indulgences. He discussed the matter by himself at home, turned over the pages of books, consulted the experts in canon law, but saw that there is nothing sound and nothing sure in indulgences. For this reason he drew up the theses: "Our Lord and Master, WATr 5:78 etc." He did not do this to attack the pope, but to oppose the blasphemous statements of the noisy declaimers. Then the whole world under Maximilian was stirred up, the pope raged, the bishops ranted that the confessional should be removed, and the Carthusians bellowed.

TABLE TALK FROM ANTON LAUTERBACH'S COLLECTION B FROM VARIOUS YEARS

WATr 5:657 6431. The beginning with Tetzel. Tetzel's abominations are plain: Indulgences are the reconciliation between God and men, what is more, they avail even if a man does not repent and is without contrition; even if anyone had impregnated the blessed Virgin Mary, he could absolve him; he also promised remission for future sins; the pope's cross when set up had power equal to that of the cross of Christ. These monstrous statements moved me to oppose him; it was WATr 5:658 not for the sake of any honor or gain. At first I prostrated myself on the ground and prayed God to be at my side. I did not yet see the great abomination of the pope but only the crass abuses. So I first wrote in suppliant fashion to the bishops of Brandenburg and Mainz that I would write against this evil if they did not remove it. The bishops sent my writing to Tetzel. After he had read it once and a second time, he is said to have shouted to his servant: "Veit, if this becomes manifest and known in Germany, the devil will really befoul us!" Then the bishops, as I had requested, sent my writing back to me. The abbot of Lehnin ordered me to be silent, but they themselves refused to be quiet and provoked me to write. And I give thanks to God, who attacked that lying realm of liars through a wretched and poor instrument like me. Still they are made weak!

John Aurifaber's Collection
(30, 7; Foerstemann-Bindseil 3, 315)

6861. Concerning the bishop of Brandenburg. Doc[tor] M[artin] WATr 6:238 L[uther] stated that when he had first begun to write against indulgences in the year 1517, he sent a letter to the bishop of Brandenburg with the request that he should restrain Tetzel. Then the bishop replied that I should not begin the business; but if I did start anything, I would have to take the full responsibility, for I was attacking the church's business. Here the devil incarnate was speaking out of this bishop.

V

Luther's Recollections

PREFACE TO THE 1538 EDITION OF THE THESES[94]

Doctor Martin Luther sends his greetings to the pious reader! WA 39/1:6

I am allowing the publication of my disputations and theses composed from the beginning of my controversy with the papacy and the dominion of the sophists, lest the magnitude of the controversy and the success God has given me in it puff me up with pride. For in these my shame is openly manifested, that is, the weakness and ignorance which in the beginning compelled me to take up the matter with the greatest of trembling and terror.

I was on my own and had slipped into the controversy inadvertently when I could not withdraw. In many important articles I was not only prepared to yield to the pope, but beyond that I even honored him. For who was I—a wretched little brother then, more like a corpse than a man—to oppose the majesty of the pontiff? Before his face not only the kings of the earth and the whole world, but heaven itself and hell—the threefold fabric of things, as the saying goes—quaked in fear and depended on his nod.

What my heart suffered quantitatively and qualitatively in that first and second year and how great was my unfeigned humility, which almost reached despair, are all too little known to those who later began to assail the majesty of the pontiff in very proud fashion, once it had been wounded! And although they did not compose these verses, to employ the words of Virgil, they have nevertheless carried off the honors, which I gladly bestowed on them.

Moreover, while they were spectators and allowed me to run risks on my own, for my part I was not so joyful, confident, and certain, for I did not know many things that I know now. Indeed, I knew nothing at all as to what indulgences were, even as the whole papacy itself did not know anything about them. They were cultivated only by usage and custom. So I did not begin to dispute in order to remove them; but since I knew pretty well what they were not, I wanted to learn what they were. And since the dead and dumb masters, that is, the books of the theologians and jurists, did not give me satisfaction, I determined to consult living men and to hear the church of God itself, so that if any organs of the Holy Spirit were left anywhere, they might have pity on me and at the same time inform me about indulgences for the common good.

At this stage many good men praised my theses. But it was impossible for me to recognize these as the church or as the organs of the Holy Spirit. I looked up to pope, cardinals, bishops, theologians, jurists, and monks as such and awaited the Spirit from them. For I was so stuffed with the drunkenness and intoxication of their doctrines that I did not know whether I was asleep or awake. And when I had overcome all arguments by means of the Scriptures, with the greatest difficulty and perplexity I just managed to get over this one difficulty with Christ supporting me: the church must be heard. Because I did it out of a true heart, I honored the church of the pope as the true church much more steadfastly and reverently than those filthy sycophants do who today make a boast of the pope's church against me. If I had despised the pope as his eulogizers now despise him, I would have thought that I should be swallowed up in the same hour with Korah and his followers.

But to return to the subject! When I awaited the opinion of the church and the Holy Spirit in this manner, silence was soon imposed on me under the sanction of custom. I yielded in terror under the authority of the prestige of the church and made the offer to keep silent to Cardinal Cajetan at Augsburg. I made the humble plea that he should likewise impose silences on the outcries of the opposing party. But he not only denied this request but added that if I did not recant, he would condemn everything I had taught. However, I had already taught the catechism with considerable success, and I knew that this should not be condemned and that I should not tolerate this unless I wished to deny Christ. So matters reached such a pass that I was compelled to make trial of desperate measure and await the outcome.

But it was not my intention at the present time to relate my history, but to confess my folly, ignorance, and infirmity, lest anyone think of me (to follow Paul) beyond what he sees in me and have no doubt—if indeed anyone could have such a doubt—that in such great difficulties I was and am a man. It was also my purpose at the same time to scare off the overbold scribblers who had no experience of the cross and Satan, those proud fellows I mean who think nothing of conquering the pope and even Satan for that matter. Luther must be the object of attack! If he is conquered, Satan is a laughing-stock to them!

What was I to do? How would it have been possible for me, even if I had been an angel, to divine that such enemies would rise up in my name behind my back? But why am I foolish enough to complain? No enemies of Christ and God have been worse than those who have persecuted Christ and God under the name of Christ and God. Read the Scriptures and you will see what happened to the prophets, apostles, and all the saints. The statement of Micah, or rather of Christ, is still true: "A man's foes are those of his own house" [Micah 7:6; Matt. 10:36]. Christ would never have been crucified if he had not nourished and raised up among the apostles the very worst of devils, Judas.

But for all that, dear brother, I confess these my infirmities and follies to you so that you, too, may learn to be wise with humility and may know for certain and in very truth that Satan is not dead but is still a prince, not of one man or of one region but of the whole world, and that there is no one who has not been subjected to his power, cunning, and ill-will except Christ alone and those who are truly Christ's.

Therefore, we have no grounds for being secure and acting 8 proudly. And we should not admire ourselves on the score of our excellent gifts over and above the rest of men. You see here—if it is permissible for me to boast at least of this—out of what great weakness the Lord brought me forth to strength, from what great ignorance He brought me forth to knowledge, and from what great trembling He brought me forth to resolution. I was certainly not without struggles and temptations, as those overbold and joyful scribblers have the effrontery to claim for themselves. And I have still not reached the point that they seem to have reached long ago. For although I do not fear the pope and his majesty now, I am still compelled to fear the pope's God almost more than at the beginning.

In short, we are nothing. Christ alone is everything. If He should turn aside His face, we should perish and Satan triumph even if we were saints, or Peters and Paul. Let us, therefore, humble our hearts under the mighty hand of God [1 Pet. 5:5] that He may exalt us in His own time. For God resists the proud but gives grace to the humble. For just as a troubled spirit is a sacrifice to God [Ps. 51:17], so without a doubt an inflexible and secure spirit is a sacrifice to the devil. Farewell in the Lord's name, and if there is need for you to do so, better yourself by my work and example.

EXHORTATION TO THE CLERGY ASSEMBLED AT THE IMPERIAL DIET AT AUGSBURG, 1530[95]

WA 30/2:278 Likewise, have you also forgotten how my teaching was at first so precious to almost all of you? Then all the bishops were very glad to see
LW 34:14 the tyranny of the pope restrained a little, since he handled the endowed foundations too severely. Then they could watch me politely,
279 listen, sit quietly, and be on the lookout how they might regain once more their entire episcopal authority. Then Luther was an excellent teacher who attacked indulgences so honestly. At that time bishops and parish priests had to put up with a monk or an intruding rascal in their chapters and parishes who with letters of indulgences carried on a thoroughly scandalous trade and no one dared to utter a sound against it. There was no doctor in all the universities or monasteries who could have known how or dared to oppose such filth. Luther was the "dear boy." He swept the chapters and parishes clean of such huckstering, held the stirrups for the bishops to enable them to

remount, and threw a stumbling block into the road for the pope. 15
Why did you not consider that revolt as well?

I heard no weeping from bishop or parish priest when afterward I
attacked the monastic life and the monks became fewer. I know that
no greater service was ever done the bishops and priests than freeing 280
them from the monks. Indeed, I fear there will now be at Augsburg
hardly anyone who will take the monks' side and ask that they return
again to their former position. No, the bishops will not allow such
bedbugs and lice to be put back in their fur again. They are happy that
I deloused their fur so thoroughly, although, to tell the truth, the
monks had to govern the church under the pope and the bishops
contributed nothing to that end except to permit themselves to be
addressed as lords. However, I have not destroyed the monks with
revolt but with my teaching and the bishops were well pleased. They
could not have done it even with the force of all the kings or with the
learning of all the universities. Why, then, did they not consider that
revolutionary, too? Ah, they are too pleased that the monks are down
and that the pope has thereby almost lost an entire hand. Still they
give no thanks to Luther, whose teaching they exploit so gloriously at
this point.

Since I now come to the point that people have forgotten how
things stood in the world before my teaching began and no one now
wants to admit to having ever done wrong, I must drag out the old 281
skeletons and place before the eyes of the clergy their forgotten virtue
so that they may see or reflect once more on what conditions would
be like in the world if our gospel had not come. We, too, may see for
our comfort what manifold glorious fruits the Word of God has produced. We wish to begin precisely at the point where my teaching
began, that is, with indulgences.

Concerning Indulgences 16

If our gospel had accomplished nothing else than to redeem consciences from the shameful outrage and idolatry of indulgences, one
would still have to acknowledge that it was God's Word and power.
For the whole world must acknowledge that no human wisdom could
have accomplished this, since no bishop, no chapter, no monastery, no
doctor, no university, not even I myself at that time, in short, no rea-

son understood or saw through this abomination. Much less did anyone know how to control or attack it, but everyone had to sanction all and let it pass for good wholesome doctrine. Also the dear bishops and popes took out their cut without blinking an eyelash and allowed it to go on full-scale, namely:

282   1. They sold the indulgence as the divine grace which forgives sin. Thereby Christ's blood and death were denied and blasphemed together with the Holy Spirit and the gospel.

2. They falsely sold souls out of purgatory through it, to the great shame of the Divine Majesty, but it brought in lots of money.

3. They thereby put the pope in heaven as a god who could command the angels to carry to heaven the souls of pilgrims who died on their trip to Rome.

4. The gospel, which is, after all, the only true indulgence, had to keep silence in the churches in deference to the indulgence.

5. Through it they defrauded and fleeced the whole world out of immeasurable sums of money with shameless greed and lies, as though they wanted to make war against the Turks.

283   6. They always declared earlier letters of indulgences void in favor of new ones and always abrogated the old indulgences in the churches for the sake of new ones, and played with the golden year, according as they wanted money. Yes, even against the Turks!

7. Also the swindle of the golden year is sheer fiction and a spurious lie to corrupt the faith of Christ and Christ's daily golden year. Yet, countless thousands of souls have been misled by it and the people shamefully duped into running to Rome, cheated of money and goods, with pains and expense lost besides.

8. In the indulgence they sold good works to all of Christendom
17   and absolution, too, as something special, which, however, the gospel forever gives the whole world free of charge. Thus consciences were led astray from the gospel and from Christ to the works of men.

9. They praised the indulgence more highly than all works of love.

10. They deposited the merit of the saints, beyond what they needed for themselves, as a treasure of indulgence, as though Christ's suf-

fering were not sufficient for the forgiveness of all sins. This again corrupts faith in Christ.

11. They finally exalted indulgence so high that they taught if some-one had even slept with the mother of God, through indulgence it would be forgiven. 284

12. They taught that when the penny rang in the money box, the soul rose to heaven.

13. One need have neither contrition nor sorrow to receive the indulgence. It was enough that one now deposit the money.

14. St. Peter himself could not grant a greater grace than the indulgence represented.

15. What has now become of the immeasurable amount of money, treasure, and wealth stolen through indulgence so long ago and acquired so shamefully?

In short, who wants to relate all the outrages that the indulgence alone brought on, as a truly mighty idol, in all the chapters, monasteries, churches, chapels, cells, altars, pictures, panels, yes, in almost all houses and chambers and wherever there was money? One would have to read anew the books that were written against it for about ten years. Now speak up, dear sirs! All of you clergy bear the guilt for this unspeakable thievery and robbery of money, for such an inconceiv- 285 able multitude of misled hearts and consciences, for such a most horrible outrageous lie and blasphemy of the suffering of Christ, of the gospel, of grace, and of God himself, perpetrated through indulgence. This is true not only of you who accepted money from it, but also of you who kept silent about it and willingly looked on at such raging of the devil. You speak of revolt, of expropriation of monasteries, of the Turks! Yes, what are all such things together compared with you indul- 18 gence hawkers, if one only wants to think of it? It was a real Turkish army against the true Christian faith.

But who among all of you would ever have repented for such frightful abomination, would ever have sighed, or would ever have moistened an eye? Yes, now, like hardened, unrepentant men you want to pretend that you never did any evil. You now come to Augsburg, therefore, and want to persuade us that the Holy Spirit is with you and will accomplish great things through you (although in your whole lifetime you have done Christendom nothing but harm) and that he will thereafter lead you straight to heaven with all such abominations, unrepented and defended besides, as though he had to rejoice over you who have served your god-belly so gloriously and laid waste his church so miserably. For this reason you have no success and also shall have none until you repent and mend your ways.

286

Well, that is one of the pretenses! That is the way things stood and went in this matter before my teaching came. That it is now that way no longer is the fault of my rebellious gospel. It is appropriate for that other trade fair called confessionals to follow the indulgence.

Concerning Confessionals

These were the butter letters in which the pope sold liberty to eat butter, cheese, milk, and eggs, and gave authority to hear mass at home, to marry within forbidden degrees, and to choose a father-confessor to release, as often as he wished, from agony and guilt in life or in perils of death and the like. My dear man, was not this, too, a blasphemous trade fair, invented in every respect for the sake of money? As if God had not before through the gospel given all such things freely to all the world, or as if God had forbidden these things, and they were the mighty men who could sell the commandments of God for money. The gospel must be nothing and God must be their merchandise. Also this swindling, bargaining, and blaspheming has been overthrown by the rebellious gospel, but now all is forgotten and there is no bishop or cleric whom it grieves or who needs forgiveness for it before God. Here, too, there was no bishop or doctor who would have condemned such matters, but all were silent and acquiesced. All right, we shall see whether, as they suppose, God will let them make a monkey of him.

287

19

Concerning Confession

Your books are still extant in which you have set down your teaching concerning confession, which I consider one of the greatest plagues on earth whereby you have confused the conscience of the whole world, caused so many souls to despair, and have weakened and quenched all men's faith in Christ. For you have said nothing at all to us about the comfort of absolution, the chief article and the best part in confession, which strengthens faith and trust in Christ. But you have made a work out of it, extorting it by force with commands from unwilling hearts to strengthen your tyranny. Afterward you let them suffer pangs, torture and torment themselves with recounting all sins. That is, you have disturbed forever their rest and peace of mind with an impossible task. But when will you bring all such souls back again and make good the deadly, baseless damage you have done? My gospel has brought to justice this kind of confession also, and strengthened once more the timid consciences. Then no bishop, doctor, or university knew anything about this and now they feel neither contrition nor sorrow for such misery. 288

Concerning Penance

That is the very worst and hell itself! If one were to forgive and remit all abominations, one can never forgive you for this one. This doctrine has filled hell and has troubled the kingdom of Christ more horribly than the Turk or the whole world could ever do. For you taught us that we should by our own works make satisfaction for sin, even against God. And that was called repenting of sin. You have nowhere given so much emphasis to contrition and confession, although you have made works of them also. Now what else does it mean to say, "You must make satisfaction for your sins," than to say, "You must deny Christ, renounce your baptism, blaspheme the gospel, 289 reproach God for lies, disbelieve the forgiveness of sins, tread underfoot Christ's blood and death, dishonor the Holy Spirit, and go to 20 heaven by your own effort with such virtues"? Alas, where are the tongues and voices which can say enough about this?

What else is such a faith than the faith of the Turks, heathen, and Jews? All of them, too, want to make satisfaction through their works. How is it possible, however, for a soul not to despair, if it has no other solace against sin than its own works? You cannot deny all this. Your books are extant in which nothing is taught about faith either in the treatment of confession or penance, but solely about our own works. Yet there is no bishop or cleric here who sheds a tear for such a monstrous, hellish blasphemy of Christ. On the contrary, they are pure and safe, while they reproach us as rebels, murder married priests, even contrary to their own law, and are annoyed because the Lutherans 290 make no pretense of fasting, as they do, and do not wear tonsures. Moreover, they defy the eternal God with all their inhuman wickedness.

From this abomination have come all the other outrages (they had to come from it, too, and there was no way of warding them off), namely, the self-righteousness of so many of the monasteries and chapters, with their worship service, the sacrificial masses, purgatory, vigils, brotherhoods, pilgrimages, indulgences, fasts, veneration of saints, relics, poltergeists, and the whole parade of the hellish proces-
21 sion of the cross. For what else is possible? If a conscience is to rely and build on its own works, it stands on loose sand which moves to and fro and continually sinks away. It must always seek works, one after the other. The longer it looks, the more it needs. At last they put cowls on the dead in which they should ascend to heaven. Dear Lord God, how were poor consciences to act? They had to build on works. Therefore, they also had to seek them so miserably and snatch whatever they could find and fall into such deep folly.

What is more, through such shameful doctrines all the legitimate
291 good works instituted and ordered by God were despised and even reduced to nothing, such as the work of a ruler, subject, father, mother, son, daughter, servant, and maid. They were not called good works and did not belong to penance either, but were known as a "secular existence," a "perilous estate," and "lost works." Thus this doctrine entirely trod under foot both the Christian and secular life and gave neither God nor Caesar his due. It invented instead a new and special life which is neither this nor that. They themselves do not know what it is, since there is no word of God for it. As Moses says, they serve gods whom they know not. That was not surprising, for at that time no one knew how to preach even the gospel in a way other than that one ought to learn from it examples and good works. None of us ever heard a gospel that was designed for the comfort of the conscience, for faith and trust in Christ, as it properly should be and, God be praised, as it is now again being preached. The world was thus in the gospel, yet was without the gospel.

If they had only wisely made a distinction with respect to satisfaction for sins, namely, that it may be made in relation to men and
292 not God, as Christ shows in Matthew 7[:12] and 18[:15]. In the past

the holy fathers, too, made use of it in this way by having Christians who had sinned make satisfaction before the congregation and the brethren, as the words suggest, and imposing two, three, or seven years of penance. Thus Christ with his satisfaction for us would still have remained in heaven. But in this way the services in the chapters and monasteries and indulgence, as I said above, would not have 22 arisen and not so much would have gotten to the great god belly. Therefore, they had to mix it all together and at last elevate satisfaction as availing only before God. This error, to be sure, assailed Christendom from the beginning, even through important men like Origen, St. Jerome, and St. Gregory, but it never reached so completely into the government of the church and to God's very throne, as happened under the pope. For this error has been the oldest from the beginning of the world. It will also probably remain the youngest until the end of the world . . .

Notes

Introduction

[1] For details, see Kurt Aland, "Die theologische Fakultät Wittenberg und ihre Stellung im Gesamtzusammenhang der Leucorea während des 16. Jahrhunderts," in his *Kirchengeschichtliche Entwürfe* (Gütersloh: Gütersloher, 1960), 283–394.

[2] WABr 1:99.8ff. (no. 41); LW 48:42 (no. 14).

[3] WATr 2:669.12 (no. 2800b).

[4] WATr 3:44.16 (no. 2871b).

[5] WATr 4:429.17 (no. 4681).

[6] Cf. "Texts," 42.

[7] Fel[ician] Gess, "Luthers Thesen und Herzog Georg von Sachsen," *Zeitschrift für Kirchengeschichte* IX (1888): 590–91; *Akten und Briefe zur Kirchenpolitik Herzog Georgs von Sachsen*, ed. Felician Gess (Leipzig: B. G. Teubner, 1905), 1:29.

[8] H[einrich] Reincke, *Hamburg am Vorabend der Reformation*, Arbeiten zur Kirchengeschichte Hamburgs 8 (Hamburg: Wittig, 1966), 64, 106; for further details, see Kurt Aland, "Der 31. Oktober als Tag des Thesenanschlags," *Kirche in der Zeit* XXI (1966): 466–69.

[9] Documentaion in Aland, "Der 31. Oktober," 467ff.

[10] WATr 5:177.29 (no. 5480).

[11] Klemens Honselmann, *Urfassung und Drucke der Ablassthesen Martin Luthers und ihre Veröffentlichung* (Paderborn: F. Schöningh, 1966). Professor Honselmann wishes to draw conclusions from the *Dialog* of Prierias of 1518 regarding the original form of the Ninety-five Theses and the story of their origin. In response only this much is to be said at the moment: The *Dialog* of Prierias definitely shows that Luther's Ninety-five Theses were a challenge for a disputation and not a petition to the bishops (*"tuis tamen verbis excitus et pene impulsus, quibus undique athletas quasi alter Dares in certamina vocas,"* Prierias said in the Introduction [Honselmann, *Urfassung und Drucke der Ablassthesen Martin Luthers*, 156, has these words separated from the actual text of the *Dialog*]). The *Dialog* also indicates that the text of the Ninety-five Theses used by Prierias agreed with the one known to us. The fact that Prierias cited only ninety-three theses and omitted those now numbered 92 and 93 is the basis for Professor Honselmann's opposing contention. A look at the wording of these (cf. p. 63) shows why Prierias did that. In contrast to the others, they do not seem to offer a starting point for an argu-

ment profitable to his point of view. Even the argument against Theses 94 and 95 is really quite general and intended only as a conclusion. In addition, Prierias also says clearly that he has skipped a few things at the end of the theses ("*Haec ergo sunt, Martine, quae ad conclusiones tuas respondenda occurrerunt, posthabitis in fine quibusdam vanis, quae loqueris*"; EA *Opera Latina var. arg.* 1:377, and for the complete text, 1:345ff.). Both citations from Prierias appear to me to make Honselmann's position, as well as the conclusions he bases on his position, untenable. Besides, the definitive versions of Theses 92 and 93 are found in Luther as early as 1516 (cf. his letter to Michael Dressel of 1516 [WABr 1:47.31ff.]), further proof to show how untenable Honselmann's theories are. In Theses 92 and 93, Luther is not adopting the thoughts of Tetzel (or Wimpina), but the latter reply to Luther. As elsewhere, too, Honselmann is confusing cause and effect.

12   Cf. "Texts," 32, 40, and *passim*.

13   Cf. pp. 81ff.

14   Cf. p. 80.

15   But perhaps also because the letter itself was written on All Saints' Day and not on 31 October. For on the festive day Luther was enjoying a glass of wine (or beer) and was recalling the preceding ten years with his friends. All Saints' Day was a festival in the Church of the Reformation for a long time, and 31 October, which fell on a Thursday in 1527, was a working day and apparently was not considered for such a gathering pp. 120–21 (cf. n. 93).

16   Cf. p. 77.

17   Cf. pp. 33, 42.

18   Cf. p. 32; similar expressions occur frequently.

19   Cf. pp. 31f., 89f., 91f.

20   Cf. p. 72. Lang could not have been the only one to whom Luther sent a copy. On the contrary, Luther spoke often of sending copies to learned men (cf. p. 74). That the accompanying letters are not extant is attributable to the fact that only a small fraction of Luther's early correspondence is preserved.

21   Cf. p. 76.

22   Cf. p. 51.

23   WATr 5:558.6ff. (no. 6250); cf. p. 102f.

24   WATr 5:138.35–139.5 (no. 5428).

25   *CR* 1:88–89.

26   *CR* 1:291; cf. also pp. 111–13 n. 50.

27   WABr 1:72.4f. (no. 28); LW 48:27 (no. 10).

28   Erwin Iserloh, *Luthers Thesenanschlag: Tatsache oder Legende?* Institut für Europäische Geschichte Mainz 31 (Wiesbaden: F. Steiner, 1962); *Luther zwischen Reform und Reformation: Der Thesenanschlag fand nicht statt*, Katholisches Leben und Kämpfen im Zeitalter der Glaubensspaltung 23/24 (Münster: Aschendorff, 1966).

29   Cf. pp. 74, 77; cf. pp. 111–13 n. 50.

30   Above all, Hans Volz, *Martin Luthers Thesenanschlag und dessen Vorgeschichte* (Weimar: Hermann Böhlaus, 1959) and its bibliography.

Texts

The texts presented in this volume were translated from the original critical texts (not from the translations of the German edition) where modern English translations were not available. The American Edition was used, unrevised and unedited, with the notes of the German edition rather than with the original footnotes of the American Edition. A complete commentary was not attempted here—that would amount to something like a summary history of the early Reformation period. Only those remarks are made that are of real interest for the special purview of this volume. For remarks of a more general nature, the reader can refer to the American Edition or the Weimar Edition.

The Ninety-five Theses and "A Sermon on Indulgence and Grace," together with source references, are conveniently accessible in their original form in vol. 142 of *Kleine Texte für Vorlesungen und Übungen: Martin Luthers 95 Thesen nebst dem Sermon von Ablass und Gnade* (separate reprint of the Luther edition by Otto Clemen, ed. Kurt Aland [Berlin: de Gruyter, 1962]). This book also contains a bibliography of the modern discussion of the Ninety-five Theses. The most important of these works and some updating of them follow:

The modern discussion began with an article by Hans Volz, "An welchem Tag schlug Martin Luther seine 95 Thesen an die Wittenberger Schlosskirche an?" *Deutsches Pfarrerblatt* LVII (1957): 457–58. The article was answered by Kurt Aland, "Der 31. Oktober 1517 gilt zu Recht als Tag des Thesenanschlages Martin Luthers," *Deutsches Pfarrerblatt* LVIII (1958): 241–45. Compare Heinrich Bornkamm, "Der 31. Oktober als Tag des Thesenanschlages," *Deutsches Pfarrerblatt* LXI (1961): 508–9.

A second phase of the discussion was opened by Erwin Iserloh, *Luthers Thesenanschlag: Tatsache oder Legende?* Institut für europäische Geschichte, Vorträge Mainz 31 (Wiesbaden: F. Steiner, 1962). This book followed an article with the same title in *Trierer theologische Zeitschrift* LXX (1961): 303–12, which in turn was evoked by Hans Volz's previously mentioned book. This independent work deals with the same material as Hans Volz cites but comes to different conclusions. Kurt Aland was also the first one to oppose Erwin Iserloh's work with "Luthers Thesenanschlag, Tatsache oder Legende?" *Deutsches Pfarrerblatt* LXII (1962): 241–44. The article also takes issue with Hans Volz once more, who had meanwhile answered Kurt Aland in another article in *Deutsches Pfarrerblatt*.

A third phase of the discussion has begun with the publications of Klemens Honselmann of Paderborn. First, he published the article "Die Veröffentlichung der Ablassthesen Martin Luthers 1517" in *Theologie und Glaube* LV (1965): 1–23. Then he published his interpretation in extended form in the book *Urfassung und Drucke der Ablassthesen Martin Luthers und ihre Veröffentlichung* (Paderborn: F. Schöningh, 1966). Especially important in this book are the facsimile reproductions of the *Dialog* of Prierias and of the Ninety-five Theses in the collected editions of 1530 and 1538. The effect of Honselmann's research will no doubt be that future editions of the Ninety-five Theses will no longer be based, as heretofore, only on the broadsheet editions but that the indirect transmission of Prierias and of the later collected editions will also be taken into consideration. But we shall have to go beyond Honselmann's suggestion. The 1531 edition of the theses (the way the 1530 edition appeared, improved, in Joseph Klug's establishment), the Basel imprint of 1538, and the *Resolutions* must also be taken into consideration if we wish to investigate the history of the text of the Ninety-five Theses and establish their original form. Moreover, we must also point out that the "Prierias edition text of the theses" (pp. i–v of the Supplement) merely looks like a facsimile. Actually it represents an artificial product. At any rate, the original Prierias editions that I have seen did not present the theses in unbroken sequence but always broken up by longer or shorter additions of Prierias. Apparently the text of the theses was snipped out of photographs of the original imprint and by means of a photograph of a paste-up made to look like continuous text.

The eventual results of the debate with Honselmann are still uncertain. For the moment the reaction is negative. Erwin Iserloh, for instance, to whom Honselmann is after all closest in his conclusions, in *Luther zwischen Reform und Reformation* (Münster: Aschendorff, 1966), 74, not only explains that he considers improbable Honselmann's contention that Luther inserted Theses 92 and 93 later; he also assembles methodological objections against Honselmann's whole approach. Similar results may be expected from further study of Honselmann's work, which in individual points, however, is certainly full of merit.

Since the summer of 1962 an extensive series of contributions to the discussion have appeared, some in church papers, some only in limited circulation publications, some in book reviews, of which only a few outstanding items can be mentioned here. An apparently complete review of all titles is to be found in Heinrich Steitz, "Luthers 95 Thesen: Stationen eines Gelehrtenstreites," *Jahrbuch der hessischen kirchengeschichtlichen Vereinigung* XIV (1963): 189–91. The most important of these are: Hans Volz, "Erzbischof Albrecht von Mainz und Martin Luthers 95 Thesen," *Jahrbuch der hessischen kirchengeschichtlichen Vereinigung* XIII (1962): 187–228; Hans Volz's own review of his book in *Luther* XXXIV (1963): 42–43 (a reply to "a review that betrayed a complete lack of interest," as Volz calls it, which appeared in the same journal, XXXIII [1962]: 143, by Hayo Gerdes); Hans Volz's review of Erwin Iserloh's book in *Theologische Literaturzeitung* LXXXIX (1964): 682–83; Franz Lau, "Zweifel um den 31. Oktober 1517?" *Lutherische Monatshefte* I (1962): 459–63; Bernhard Lohse, "Der Stand der Debatte über Luthers Thesenanschlag," *Luther* XXXIV (1963): 132–36. In addition to these, Martin Schmidt made the statement that he had been incorrectly noted by Lohse as agreeing with Iserloh. Schmidt said, "The final result remains the same: no Protestant church historian has been convinced by Erwin Iserloh's argument against the posting of the theses" (*Luther* XXXV [1964]: 48). At the twenty-sixth convention of German historians (Berlin, 7–11 October 1964), a discussion of the posting of the theses was carried on by Iserloh, Volz, and Aland. The essays together with a bibliography by Heinrich Steitz and a summary by J. Höss of the results of the discussion have been published in *Geschichte in Wissenschaft und Unterricht* XVI (1965): 661–99. This report presents a comprehensive survey of the state of the discussion at that time. Further works on the subject (for example, by Heinrich Bornkamm) are in the press. A review of the progress of the whole debate and of its results is being prepared by Kurt Aland ("Die 95 Thesen Martin Luthers: Ein Überblick über die Resultate der gegenwärtigen Diskussion," which is scheduled to appear in *Zeitschrift für Kirchengeschichte*). The earlier definitive research by Johannes Luther, *Vorbereitung und Verbreitung von Martin Luthers 95 Thesen* (Berlin: de Gruyter, 1933), has now been superseded by the aforementioned book by Hans Volz, *Martin Luthers Thesenanschlag und dessen Vorgeschichte* (Weimar: Hermann Böhlaus, 1959). The latter work assembles and examines the scattered and not easily accessible material. Even for those who cannot agree with Volz's opinion that the posting of the theses did not occur on 31 October but on 1 November, this book remains the starting point for working on the Ninety-five Theses.

Luther's Preface to Volume 1 of His Latin Writings, Wittenberg Edition, 1545

1 The Wittenberg Edition was named after its place of origin, as has been the custom frequently in Luther editions. It began to appear in 1539 with volume 1 of the German series. Not until 1545 did volume 1 of the Latin series follow and in 1546 volume 2 of this series (with Melanchthon's introduction, pp. 44ff.). Finally in 1548 volume 2 of the German series appeared.

2 "Texts," pp. 69ff.

3 Not extant and could not be located already in 1545.

4 "Texts," pp. 55ff.

5 "Texts," pp. 63ff.

6 "Texts," pp. 78ff., the first part of the introduction addressed to Pope Leo X.

7 In July 1518; his initiation lecture was on 29 August 1518.

8 Emperor Maximilian I died on 12 January 1519; Luther probably got the news somewhat later, which accounts for his dating.

9 This happened in 1520: The bull threatening excommunication was signed on 15 June 1520; the conversations to which Luther makes reference took place in November 1520.

10 That is, 1519; after the excursus into the year 1520—motivated by the thought that the papal excommuniction was gradually losing credit—Luther returns to the chronological exposition. The excursus stemmed from the thought that the papal ban gradually lost all prestige.

11 On 27 June 1519 the debate was begun, and from 4 July on, Luther and Eck debated.

12 In January in Altenburg.

13 Not extant.

14 The second series of lectures on Psalms is meant; the dedicatory introduction to the first fascicle of the imprint is dated 27 March 1519.

15 1515–1516.

16 1516–1517.

17 1517–1518. Luther's subsequent discussion of his "tower experience," that is, his breakthrough to the Reformation understanding of the justification of sinful man through God's grace alone, have been the subject of an extraordinary volume of discussion. Earlier scholars believed that Luther is here indicating a point of time before or even during his first Psalm lectures (1513–1514), but Ernst Bizer and

others have supported a date before the second series of Psalm lectures (1518–1519). Compare Kurt Aland, *Der Weg zur Reformation: Zeitpunkt und Charakter des reformatorischen Erlebnisses Martin Luthers*, Theologische Existenz, N. F., 123 (Munich: C. Kaiser, 1965).

[18] The reference is to chapters 9 and 11 of St. Augustine's *De spiritu et littera*.

[19] The printed second Psalms lectures go only as far as Psalm 22. Here Luther had to stop. The Imperial Diet of Worms was called for 6 January 1521, but the announcement of its convening was dated 1 November 1520. This is also the year of the debate whether Luther should be invited to the imperial diet. In December 1520, Luther said he would go there under any conditions, even if he were ill.

"Against Hanswurst, 1541"

This work belongs to a series of writings originating in the sharp literary clash that pitted Duke Henry of Braunschweig-Wolfenbüttel against Landgrave Philip of Hesse and Elector John Frederick of Saxony. Luther became involved in the debate through Henry's attack on his elector and incidentally on his own person. The controversy as such is not of interest for the present discussion. The essay contains other important matters, too, but the excerpt reproduced here is a self-contained unit.

[20] That is, Archbishop Albert of Mainz, whom Luther also attacks in this work.

[21] Lutheran tumult.

[22] That is, the duke of Braunschweig.

[23] Luther's promotion to doctor of theology had taken place on 18/19 October 1512.

[24] Luther had preached against indulgence on 27 July 1516, on 31 October 1516 (!), and on 24 February 1517.

[25] *Instructio summaria*; cf. "Texts," p. 71.

[26] "Texts," pp. 69ff. Albert was archbishop of Mainz and Magdeburg and bishop of Halberstadt.

[27] Both letters are not extant.

[28] The Dominican order; Tetzel, too, was a Dominican.

[29] Eck.

[30] *Dreketen* is a pun on *Dekreten* ("decrees") and *Dreck* ("dirt"), which Luther used often. Luther's essay is couched in passionate terms; even the title—"Against Hanswurst"—betrays that quality. But to say the least, the previous works of his opponents show at least the same intensity of language.

[31] See "Texts," pp. 78ff., for the beginnings of it.

[32] Albert of Mainz; Heinz, or "Harry," is Henry of Braunschweig.

[33] The citation arrived in Wittenberg on 7 August 1518. The papal brief *Postquam ad aures* with the accompanying briefs came on 23 August 1518. It ordered the heretic to be tied hand and foot and jailed until further instruction arrived. Between 7 and 23 August are 16 days. Therefore, Luther was either wrong or should have written "16 days later"; or else he meant another incident about which he might have heard some proven or false oral report, perhaps about the consultations that

preceded the issuance of the briefs. At any rate, it cannot be attributed to a mere slip of the pen because Luther used this phrase frequently, for example, in his Table Talk.

34 On 28 November 1518. The text is given in WA 2:36–40.

35 A release from ecclesiastical punishments.

36 From Simon Magus (Acts 8:18ff.), who wanted to buy the gift of bestowing the Holy Spirit.

37 Deeds such as Judas Iscariot's.

Melanchthon's Preface to Volume 2 of Luther's Latin Writings, Wittenberg Edition, 1546

38 Cf. "Texts," p. 39.

39 What Melanchthon demands here for Luther we should also let stand for Melanchthon himself and should not reject his biographical data without cogent reasons. A few little errors—Luther himself committed errors when he spoke about his life—do not vitiate the reliability of the whole story. We know that Melanchthon, who himself taught history, was very much interested in the details of Luther's life. Melanchthon was not satisfied to have only Luther describe the course of his career to him (WATr 5:538 [no. 6250], Luther said: "I have often discussed these matters with Melanchthon and reported to him the beginning and the story of my lifetime"). Melanchthon made inquiries also of Luther's mother concerning the date of his birth and concerning his youth. From the summer of 1518 on, he himself was involved in all that happened and stood in close relation to all persons who affected Luther's life. The events of that and the following year still had close connection with the Ninety-five Theses. When Melanchthon came to Wittenberg, Luther was preparing for the trip to Augsburg for consultation with Cajetan. Melanchthon maintained a very close connection with the faculty as well as the students of the university. They could give him very accurate information about the year of the indulgence controversy, which he had not personally witnessed. Actually it was less than ten months from 31 October 1517 to the arrival of Melanchthon in Wittenberg. Anyone who is newly called to a university investigates its current problems and its history as well as the biography of the important colleagues with whom he will associate to get a picture of the situation as quickly and reliably as possible—especially if he has historical interests. In August 1518, the scandal of Luther was already a very important issue. Just then we see him in close contact with Melanchthon, who considers himself a partisan in the discussions in a very short time—in short, it is not conceivable that Melanchthon was *not* informed soon after his arrival of the details of the indulgence controversy, such as the history of the Ninety-five Theses. We might even consider the possibility that he knew about it before he came to Wittenberg.

40 This assurance underscores the previous arguments.

41 The special interest of Melanchthon regarding the birthday probably stems from his inclinations toward astrology. But his frequent inquiries of the family, and not just of one member of it, point to his lively interest in Luther's complete biog-

raphy; it is especially his own personal investigations that often stand behind the next episodes of his narration.

42 That controversy (cf. "Texts," pp. 40ff.) accepts the reproach about the beginnings of the Lutheran tumult.

43 Further chiefly essential considerations, for which there is not room here, follow (CR 6:164–70).

The Ninety-five Theses, 1517

44 We still have two broadsheets of the Ninety-five Theses. One was printed in Nuremberg and is extant in two copies. The other comes from Leipzig and is extant in three copies, one of which has been lost since World War II. We have no copy of the original Wittenberg broadsheet or of their probably immediate reprints. Only the reprint from Basel in book form is available in larger numbers of copies. All three extant imprints were obviously composed independently of each other. That so many more copies are extant in book form is explained by the fact that it was better adapted for storage, while the broadsheets (about 10 x 15) were necessarily folded for storage. Then they were often torn at the folds and fell into four parts, which were easily lost. The copies of the original Wittenberg imprint were also probably rather few in number. Luther paid for the printing and needed only one copy for posting and a few more for sending out. Thus not a single copy is extant or is even known to have existed—an illustration of what was said about the "prehistorical period" of the Reformation (pp. 20–21).

45 Crassus (d. 53 B.C.) has the cognomen "the Rich" because of his wealth and has become the prototype of the rich man.

46 If the theses are read in succession, it becomes clear at latest in the second part that as far as Luther was concerned they were not merely to be presented to the bishops, as Iserloh has it. Rather, the intent was that they be a document to evoke (public) debate. In writing them down, the author already thought of the public that would attend the debate and presented his arguments accordingly. This becomes clear thesis by thesis from Thesis 42 on. Iserloh supposes "that as far as he [Luther] was concerned, something else was at stake than a debate at the University of Wittenberg" (27). In regard to what Luther said about the theses, "it is enough to accept the fact that Luther on 31 October sent the theses to the appropriate representatives of the church" (19). Luther chose the thesis format even though he "was not in fact thinking of one of the customary debates" because "this form allowed him to express opinions disputandi causa ["for purposes of debate"] without identifying himself with them" (31). Now, Luther did not think of the theses in so detached a way because in the Resolutions he defends them all emphatically and does not drop a single one of them expressly. To be precise, Luther was concerned not about a matter of style but about a fundamental clarification of the indulgence question. This could never be achieved by sending the theses to the bishops. Only in a discussion of the matter, in a debate, could this take place, either in person or, in case personal meetings were impossible, in writing. The introduction to the theses is clear enough. It constitutes a challenge to debate. If this expression of challenge was

made only for appearance's sake, for camouflage—as Iserloh's theory compels one to suppose—why the artificial cloak of a differentiation between present and absent participants, between oral or written debate? It would have been sufficient to choose the customary form of thesis introduction, that is, to limit oneself to the first sentence; in that case the second sentence of the introduction would have been completely superfluous. Luther sent his *Resolutions*, that is, his clarification and proof for the Ninety-five Theses, to Bishop Jerome Schulz before their publication (p. 74). But the argument should not be used that he had done the same thing with the Ninety-five Theses. Between the theses and *Resolutions* lay four months in which Luther had suffered the heaviest attacks. Seeing that his reputation in the church was already ruined among many people and that the danger to his own person had already increased considerably, Luther had to consider how he might approach the appropriate ecclesiastical authority with new publications to provide, if possible, a defense or at least to prevent increased opposition. Besides, we must not overlook the fact that the theses in the Weimar Edition cover six pages, but the *Resolutions* cover no less than 104 pages! The two cannot be considered together in the way it is often done in present-day discussions. Ecclesiastically speaking, the Luther of spring and summer 1518 is not to be likened to the Luther of 31 October 1517. On 31 October 1517 he still stands before his "fall into sin." In 1518, he has experiences and events behind him of which he had as yet no conception at the earlier date. Only in and after the consultation with Cajetan do his opinions about the church change. He gains a determination and a sense of assurance in his growing dissociation from the organized church, as that church faced him in Cajetan and Prierias, such as he does not have in the spring of 1518. He was, of course, not anticatholic and antipapist yet, but his devotion to the church and her institutions was gradually beginning to diminish.

"A Sermon on Indulgence and Grace, 1518"

47 Here in the last paragraph the temporal—and material—cleavage between the sermon and the Ninety-five Theses becomes clear. The extant imprints carry the date 1518, and the sermon probably appeared in February/March 1518. At any rate, in the second half of March it was already in existence (Luther to Spalatin, WABr 1:161–62 [no. 67]). Luther expressed his desire to Scheurl on 5 March 1518 to write a German piece that might take the place of the Ninety-five Theses for the church (p. 76), and one is led to suppose that he had this sermon in mind. Of course, the sermon would then have had to be written down in an extremely short period of time after this letter (that would pose no difficulty, considering the speed of Luther's production) and printed (the chief drawback for this theory lies in the slowness of printing and the printers at that time; then there is still the question whether Luther would have called the little sermon a "booklet" [*libellus*]).

To Albert of Mainz, 31 October 1517

48 "A Sermon on Indulgence and Grace" already constituted a commentary on the Ninety-five Theses. This letter gives us an indication of the situation in which

Luther composed the Ninety-five Theses. Obviously they were written down not on 31 October 1517 but actually some time before that. Their composition may have taken considerable time; moreover, preliminary sketches for them may have been done first and so on. An artistically constructed series of theses ninety-five statements long requires careful deliberation and has to take account of the theories of many potential opponents. It is not completed in a first draft. So the composition of the theses took place in the month of October, their beginnings perhaps as early as the first half of the month. They still had to be printed before posting (unless Luther posted them in manuscript, which is not probable, all things considered). The printer, too, necessarily had to have a certain amount of time for preparing the broadsheet of the Ninety-five Theses.

This letter Luther saved—something that very seldom happened otherwise. Not only did he write in the letter to Frederick the Wise in November 1518 (p. 80) that it still existed, but even in 1541 (p. 41), he still had it at his disposal. Luther said in 1518 the letter had "gone through many hands." That is really what happened. We know, for example, of a copy of Luther's letter that Deacon John Dietrich took to Thorn, where he worked from 1515 to 1519 (WABr 1:109). Therefore, by 1519 copies of the letter had already reached Thorn (modern Torun, Poland).

We can report even more about this letter—such are the vagaries of chance. By amazing coincidence the original is extant. It is located in the Royal Archives in Stockholm, where it arrived after its release in 1694 from the estate of Superintendent Theodore Schultz of Ösel. How he ever got possession of the letter cannot even be conjectured. The original still bears the chancery mark. The mark indicates that the secretaries of Albert opened the missive in Calbe on 17 November 1517 (therefore, about a week after Luther had sent the theses to Lang). Albert was not in Calbe at the time but at his residence in Aschaffenburg, where the secretaries immediately forwarded the letter together with an enclosure. Apparently there were even two enclosures, for Albert confirmed the arrival on 13 December 1517 of a "tract and thesis of an impudent monk of Wittenberg." But the tract would presumably refer to Luther's "Tractatus de indulgentiis," not his "Sermon on Indulgence and Grace." Several matters remain in the dark here: the long period of time between the sending and the opening of the letter in Calbe. It must have arrived there at the latest by 2 November because the distance between Wittenberg and Calbe is not considerable (42 miles). Did the secretaries let it lie unopened so long? Was it because they were perhaps awaiting the momentary return of the archbishop? Luther further states again and again (pp. 33, 41, and in the following letters and Table Talk) that he wrote two letters: one to Albert and the other to Bishop Jerome of Brandenburg. We have precise information about the first one; about the second we know nothing at all. Efforts have been made to explain this by the theory that the letters were identical in wording. Only for the one sent to Mainz did Luther make a draft for himself or even take a copy of it. This copy he saved. His statements about the letter can refer only to this copy, for the original was obviously filed in one of the archives of Cardinal Albert. The one to the Brandenburg bishop, it is assumed, he copied directly either from the letter to Albert or from his own draft. This is possible, but Luther then had to change the text considerably from the copy. A reading of the letter indicates that a series of expressions in it refer only to Albert. The commission for the indulgence preachers had appeared under his name, not under the Brandenburg bishop's.

[49] Further, a simple reading of the letter also indicates that certain deductions made from the letter are not warranted. This is true in the first place of the opinion that "the excessive, sweeping protestations of devotion and humility of the accompanying letter" would appear "to border on poor taste," as Karl-August Meissinger has it (Iserloh, p. 33 [this citation refers to his booklet of 1962, as it opened the debate]). Iserloh concurs and even thinks that these expressions "were lies," that is, in case Luther had actually posted the theses. The truth is that the sixteenth-century style of letter writing was different from ours. A person only has to read how the humanists wrote to each other, referring to themselves in diminutives and raising others high with superlatives (if there were a superlative form of this word, we should have to use it here). Here the border of poor taste often was not just reached but even crossed, for obviously only the vanity of the addressee was being appealed to. When Luther, an unknown Augustinian monk and a professor of a tiny university (p. 12), wrote to the Hohenzollern Cardinal Albert, archbishop of Mainz and thus primate of the German church, archchancellor of the German empire and presiding officer of the college of electors, archbishop of Magdeburg, and bishop of Halberstadt, then the expressions of devotion of the first part of the letter were not only a matter of contemporary style but an expression of the real difference in station and of the feeling of devotion of "the totally mad papist" over against the highest dignitary of the church in Germany. But this feeling of devotion is limited by the demands of conscience and the dire needs of the church, as Luther understands them. From the second paragraph on, the letter becomes not only businesslike but also pointed and in its demands even rather extreme. After all, Luther calls for nothing less from the cardinal than the revocation of the *Instruction* that went out to the indulgence preachers under his name and an order that would completely change their entire practice. Albert obviously did not get the impression that the letter was excessively devoted and humble, for he speaks of "an impudent monk."

[50] And finally: a reading of the letter establishes the impression received already in the study of the Ninety-five Theses themselves. Iserloh's theory cannot be correct. If the theses had been composed to be sent to the ecclesiastical authorities and not for posting and as the basis for a debate, Luther's letter would have said something else. Then the presentation of the theses and the purpose of the presentation would have been revealed and justified in the body of the letter. The entire letter would have been pointed in that direction. But in reality Luther does not mention the theses until after the letter has been finished and the date already recorded— in a postscript just before attaching his signature. The sending of the theses is not the reason for the letter; it is a side issue, a matter of incidental information, you might say. To be sure, it would have been very unusual to send such theses for a debate to a bishop except for the purpose of drawing him, as it were, into the circle of scholars to whom these theses were exclusively addressed. Apparently Iserloh's conception of the posting of the theses is strongly influenced by the historical painters or by the view current in nineteenth-century Protestant circles (Reformation festivals!). He writes:

> In this connection it appears to me to be important whether Luther did or did not post the theses amid the traffic of pilgrims to All Saints Church; that is, whether he made a scene or forwarded the theses solely to bishops and a few learned men: to the former, that they might correct the abuse, to the latter that they might clarify the theological questions that were still open.

Similarly he wrote (p. 33): "If Luther would have made a scene of posting theses on 31 October 1517. . . ." Posting theses is a very normal activity in a university city that occurs a number of times every week. It takes place outside the sphere of simple men, even if they observe the act. What is posted that way is in Latin; and even if the man can read, he can probably not read Latin texts. If Luther posted the theses, he aimed at the theologians and learned visitors who could be expected to come from Wittenberg and environs to the high festival of the Castle Church in no small numbers. Therefore, it is also conceivable that he did the posting before the service and festivities began, that is, before noon, or at least around noontime. There was no "scene." It was just as normal as that a person did not propose theses to a bishop for approval. In his introduction to the *Resolutions* addressed to Pope Leo X, Luther refers to the fact that his debate about indulgences agrees with the "custom of all universities and of the entire church" and that he had the right to debate far more important matters than indulgences, a privilege granted him as a professor of theology by the pope himself. Here again Luther speaks of a "debate," not of a statement to the bishops, whose competence, together with that of all other offices, for such discussion is the very subject of dispute. Even in the case of a series of propositions of whose explosive nature he was certain and from which he hoped for significant results he did not think of submitting them anywhere for approval but made the theses known in the usual manner: by posting them and by sending copies to those colleagues and friends whom he hoped to spur on to a discussion about the issues or even to a formal debate. That is the way he had handled the matter of his exceedingly harsh debate against Scholastic theology as recently as September 1517. This disputation had violently opposed both the scholarly and the ecclesiastical authorities of the time.

That the Ninety-five Theses were understood by contemporaries as a summons to the disputation is clearly seen from the exchange of letters between the theological faculty of Mainz and Albrecht of Mainz. For his case against Luther, Albrecht wanted to have the opinion of the faculty, and for this purpose he sent his secretary, Lorcher, to them on 1 December 1517. The faculty, however, hesitated. Thus Albrecht, in a letter of 11 December, admonishes them. Even here the *Conclusiones*, that is, disputation theses, are mentioned twice. The opinion of the faculty, which finally came on 17 December 1517, even says that at the University of Wittenberg they were "disputed publicly and in scholarly fashion" ("*Conclusiones seu positiones in insigne universali gymnasio Wittenburgensi scholastice et publice disputatas*"). These texts, which have so far not been used in the discussion, were published as far back as 1902 by Hermann, *Zeitschrift für Kirchengeschichte* 23, 266f. From this, to be sure, it cannot be inferred that the disputation actually took place, the faculty of Mainz simply concluded this from the introduction to the theses. For their evaluation they had either the original document Luther sent to Albrecht or a copy made from it. A more decisive proof that the theses were really written for a disputation, and that the opinion of Iserloh is false, can hardly be imagined.

Iserloh, in the meantime, has essentially changed his original position. Astoundingly enough, he explains in his book *Luther zwischen Reform und Reformation* (1966): "that does not deprive them (the theses) of their inner adaption for a disputation, which I have never denied." Indeed, he goes so far as to say: "He who cannot reconcile himself to do without this (i.e., a posting of the theses) may place it in the middle of November, around the time the theses were sent to John Lang" (80). That this late date is impossible hardly needs to be proved. Luther's letter to Spalatin from the early part of November (p. 71) already shows that the Ninety-five Theses were known and discussed in Wittenberg long before the "middle of November." (Moreover, the letter to Lang was written on 11 November, that is definitely before the "middle of November.") Spalatin, who was not at Wittenberg but at the court at Lochau, clearly knows about the theses immediately after 31 October, for, at the latest on 5 November, Luther answers the inquiry of Spalatin why he had not sent the theses to the court. This can be explained only if the theses were posted on 31 October so copies could be made from it, through which the theses became generally know in Wittenberg and beyond.

[51] For Volz, too, this letter to Albert of Mainz plays a special role. From this letter, he supposes, Melanchthon reconstructed the date of 31 October 1517 for the posting of the theses. From his exposition, one gathers that Volz argues for Melanchthon's acquaintance with this letter only after Luther's death (also Iserloh, p. 23). With this assumption Volz's theory was conceivable: Melanchthon knew nothing of the posting of the theses and the date of the posting from firsthand knowledge. In 1545, when he learned of Luther's letter with the date of 31 October 1517 from the first volume of the Wittenberg Edition, in which the Ninety-five Theses were also printed, the two items became associated in his way of looking at them, and he dated the posting of the theses as he did it in Luther's biography (p. 51). If Volz now states he did not assume that Melanchthon did not learn about the letter until after Luther's death, then the proof of his thesis becomes even more difficult than before. Indeed, it is almost certainly to be assumed that Melanchthon learned of the letter much earlier. If Luther explained in November 1518 (when Melanchthon was in Wittenberg four months already) that his letter to Albert was extant and had already passed through many hands (p. 80), then it is to be supposed that Melanchthon of all people does not belong among those who knew nothing about it. At Luther's table not only newly forwarded letters were analyzed and discussed but also important letters of earlier time. And of all people Melanchthon, interested as he was in history and biography, should not have informed himself about the details of this activity? We know that Melanchthon learned of the theses much earlier. And it could not have been otherwise, for the discussions of 1519 were still directly related to them. In his report on the Leipzig Disputation, which Melanchthon composed in letter form and sent to Oecolampadius on 21 July 1519 (and had printed a little later!), Melanchthon said that Luther had posted propositions for debate (!) about indulgences in the previous year (*CR* 1:89). In his apology for Luther of 1521, his very statements about the theses have the ring of the heading of the theses about them. From the very beginning, Melanchthon

was informed about the theses—and no doubt about their early history.

The Wittenberg Edition itself proves that the theory of Volz cannot be correct. In the first volume of the Latin series of 1545, at the margin of the text of the letter of 31 October 1517, we read: *"Lutheri Epistola missa Kalend. novembr. anno 1517 ad cardinalem archiepiscopum Moguntinum &c. una cum propositionibus de poeitentia & indulgentiis tum primum editis"* ("Luther's letter sent on the Calends [i.e., the first] of November in the year 1517 to the cardinal archbishop of Mainz together with the theses on penance and indulgences first edited then"). Wilhelm Ernst Tentzel indicated that already 250 years ago in *Historischer Bericht*, ed. Ernst Salomon Cyprian [Leipzig: Gleditsch & Weidmann, 1717; 2d ed.], 264). The Wittenberg Edition, from which Melanchthon got his information, according to Volz, attributes the sending of the letter to 1 November 1517. If Melanchthon set the date on 31 October, he must have gone back to other sources.

To George Spalatin, First Days of November 1517

[52] George Spalatin (real name, John Burkhard) was born 17 January 1484 near Nuremberg in Spalt (hence his name), secretary and court preacher of Frederick the Wise, very influential, a close friend of Luther (more than 400 of Luther's letters to him are extant; if Luther would have been as careful with Spalatin's letters as Spalatin was with his, we should know far more about the Reformation's early history).

[53] For the date of this letter, cf. 114–15 n. 58.

[54] This concerns a satire of Pope Julius II credited to Erasmus; it circulated in manuscript form.

[55] Does he mean Albert of Mainz or the indulgence preachers?

[56] The preceding statements are probably to be interpreted as follows: The indulgence issue had beside the ecclesiastical and religious sides also a thoroughly political side; the numerous offices of Albert (archbishop of Mainz, archbishop of Magdeburg, bishop of Halberstadt) indicate an essential strengthening of the power of the Hohenzollerns (Albert's brother, Joachim I, was elector of Brandenburg). Consequently, these offices already threatened Frederick the Wise, who understandably had forbidden indulgence selling in his land. The danger of political alliances, which Luther wished to avoid, in fact lay close at hand. Even later Luther had to defend himself against this danger. (See p. 80.)

[57] In letters to his friends Lang and Spalatin in these years, Luther used this form of his name Hellenized in humanist fashion (*Eleutherius* means a free man, or a liberal-minded person).

[58] The promise was made a year prior to this. Luther inquires of Spalatin in this letter about the "clothes" (i.e., a habit or the material for one) and immediately afterward inquires the same thing of the elector. On 11 November, he can gratefully assure Spalatin that he had received it. Therefore, he received it at the latest on this day or more probably earlier. Consequently, the dating of this letter the very first days of November is certain. Because Luther at the same time answers Spalatin's question about the theses, the latter must have found out about them immediately after 31 October; and that indeed, not from Luther, but from a third party.

To John Lang, 11 November 1517

59 John Lang (ca. 1488–1548), doctor and professor of theology at Erfurt, from 1519 district vicar (as Luther's successor) of the Augustinian Eremite order, close friend of Luther.

60 Here Luther alludes to the sending of the ninety-seven theses Against Scholastic Theology, which came two months before. He had entrusted them to a master who was just then going from Wittenberg to Erfurt, but in the haste of the messenger's departure, Luther had not been able to include a letter. He sent the letter later on 4 September 1517 (WABr 1:103 [no. 45]):

> Through Master Otto I have sent you our theses and my interpretation of the Ten Commandments. I did not have enough time then to enclose a letter because I was told he was leaving immediately. Incidentally, I am exceedingly, overly, strongly, anxiously awaiting your reaction to our paradoxes. I actually suspect that what cannot be anything but orthodox to our men appears to your men to be a paradox—no! even cacodox ["heretical"].

> Do this favor for me as quickly as you can and be sure to show this at my behest to my Lord and indeed to the reverend fathers of the theological faculty and to any others whom you would advise. Indicate that I am surely most ready to come and debate the theses publicly either in the college or in the monastery. Do not let them think I wish to mutter to myself in a corner, if indeed our university is so insignificant as to be thought of as a corner.

61 The fear expressed in Luther's letter of September 1517 came to be reality in every respect; the letter to his teacher in Erfurt, Trutfetter (p. 77), is eloquent testimony to the same effect.

62 Latin: "*de ipsis editionibus meis vel conclusionibus quid sentiant*" ("what they think about my publications or conclusions [theses] themselves"), and shortly thereafter: "*Non itaque volo . . . ut prius eorum consilio et decreto mihi utendum esse credant, quam edam*" ("I do not want . . . that they should believe I should make use of their advice and decision before I go into publication"). In connection with the thesis debate, the meaning of *edere* ("to publish") has been argued much. According to these two citations, it appears at any rate that Luther at the moment of the letter thinks of the publication of the theses either as already completed or as imminent. If one considers this letter to Spalatin (p. 71), in which he says of the theses: "*a me fuisse editas*," then only the first opinion is possible.

To Jerome Schulz, Bishop of Brandenburg, 13 February 1518

63 The essential information about this letter has already been given on p. 25. As you read the letter, you almost get the impression that this is a preface to the *Resolutions*, similar to the one written for Pope Leo X (p. 78). But that is not actually the case, as the following letter to Scheurl proves. Luther has just sent to the bishop the manuscript of his *Resolutions* to the Ninety-five Theses, that is, the commentary to them, in which each thesis is documented and defended in detail.

[64] All that happened before the composition of the Ninety-five Theses.

[65] ". . . *sed interim de tanta re disputare*"—not even an indication that the theses were thought of as a communication to the prelates. The addressee is one of those to whom this information allegedly was directed.

[66] "*Itaque emisi disputationem.*"

[67] Compare p. 55, the heading of the theses.

[68] There follows an excursus on the bases of theological argumentation.

[69] The following letters serve as a commentary to this.

To Christoph Scheurl, 5 March 1518

[70] Christoph Scheurl was professor of law, rector, and dean of the law faculty at the University of Wittenberg 1507–1512, then legal adviser of his home town Nuremberg.

[71] Probably prints.

[72] According to Kurt Aland, "Der 31. Oktober," 468f., a completely new reconstruction is possibly presented. The conclusions drawn from the letter of 5 March 1518 are, in his opinion, incorrect, or at least inadequate. Already in 1930, Otto Clemen, it seems to him, stated it correctly in a few plain words: "The theses of Luther that Scheurl sent to Truchsess, Kilian Leib, and Eck on 5 November are not also the ones he sent to Franz Günther, but rather the Ninety-five." This remark is hidden in a note on Scheurl's letter to Luther of 3 November 1517 (WABr 1:116 n. 9) and, therefore, apparently has not been noted sufficiently up to this time. The situation is actually rather complicated. Scheurl and Luther were maintaining a constant exchange of ideas and writings at the time in which we are interested. The course of events went as follows:

a. On 11 September 1517 Luther sent Scheurl the theses Against Scholastic Theology and told him he could also make them accessible to Eck (WABr 1:106).

b. On 30 September 1517 Scheurl replied that he would send the disputation Against Scholastic Theology not just to Eck but also to the theologians of Cologne and Heidelberg (WABr 1:107).

c. On 3 November 1517 Scheurl wrote to Luther that his theses (Against Scholastic Theology) "*decano Eystetensi, homini erudito, et plerisque aliis probantur*" ("are approved by Dean Truchsess of Eichstadt, a learned gentleman, and many other people") (WABr 1:116).

d. On 5 November 1517 Scheurl wrote to Truchsess: "*Interea mitto tibi ac amicis communibus d. Eckio et priori Kiliano propositiones vere theologicas et admirandas, unde auctoritate tua dignas sum arbitratus*" ("Meanwhile I am sending you and our mutual friends Dr. Eck and Prior Kilian some truly theological and wonderful theses; I think they deserve your authoritative judgment") (*Christoph Scheurls Briefbuch*, ed. Franz Freiherrn von Soden and Joachim R. F. Knaake [Potsdam: Gropius, 1869–1872], 2:39). If Scheurl already on 3 November indicated to Luther the agreement of Truchsess with the theses Against Scholastic Theology, he could not send them to Truchsess as late as 5 November. Therefore, he must have been referring to other *propositiones* of Luther, namely, the Ninety-five Theses. To prove that Scheurl was moved by a specific new impression and was not speaking of something familiar to him for almost two months already, note that he sent the theses to Kilian Leib in Rebdorf and Johann Eck in Ingolstadt *on the very same day*. To Lieb he wrote: "*Quum autem amicitiam tuam non vulgarem honorem arbitrer et eam perpetuari velim, mitto ad te amici mei theology Luder propositiones quasdam, confisus illas tibi minime absurdas futuras*" ("But since I consider your friendship an uncommon honor and wish it to continue, I am sending you certain theses of my theologian friend Luther and trust that they will be far from disagreeable to you") (*Briefbuch*, 39). To Eck: "*Conclusiones iuridicas misi Vittenb., unde alias sed vere Christianas et plane theologicas accepi, quas decano Eichstetensi et priori in Rebdorff tibi communicandas transmisi. Quid de his sentias cupio cum Martino Luder reddi certior*" ("I have sent the law theses of Wittenberg; from there I have received other theses, but truly Christian and plainly theological ones, which I have sent to Dean Truchsess of Eichstadt and the Prior in Rebdorf to be shared with you. With Martin Luther I should like to know what you think of them") (*Briefbuch*, 40). Scheurl is obviously conscious of being able to offer something new and special.

e. On 5 January 1518 Scheurl thanks Ulrich Dinstedt for the receipt of a copy of the theses: "*Conclusiones Martinianas grato animo accepi, quas nostri traduxere et in pretio habent*" ("I am grateful to have received Martin Luther's theses, which our people have translated and have for sale") (*Briefbuch*, 42). From this some people have tried to deduce the date of Scheurl's first acquaintance with the Ninety-five Theses. But that appears to be incorrect. Something else is said in the text: the "*nostri traduxere et in pretio habent*" ("our people *have* translated") rather points to the fact that Scheurl has learned nothing new here. In a rather condescending manner he points out that Dinstedt's news is already stale among the Nurembergers. On that same day he could also speak to Trutfetter in Eisenach about the theses as familiar to both of them for a long time: "*arbitror legisse te apologiam Erasmi contra Stapulensem super versu: Minuisti eum paulo minus ab angelis, pariter et conclusiones Martini Luderi indulgentias interpretant*" ("I believe you *have read* Erasmus' defense against Lefèvre on the passage 'Thou madest Him a little lower than the angels' and likewise the theses of Martin Luther discussing indulgences") (*Briefbuch*, 41). What Dinstedt sent to Scheurl could have been the recent edition of the Ninety-five Theses in book form that Adam Petri prepared at the end of 1517 in Basel. Bernhard Adelmann, for instance, expresses gratitude on 11 January 1518 for the receipt of such a book but explains that he had received it from Basel even earlier (Franz H. Thurnhofer, *Bernhard Adelmann von Adelmannsfelden* [Freiburg: Herder, 1900], 58).

f. This follows from the fact that Scheurl could send copies of the Nuremberg edition of the theses already on 5 and 8 January 1518. In a letter to Peutinger, he restricted himself to information about the sending of the theses: "*mitto conclusiones amici Martini Luderi theologi quas auctoritate tua dignas sum arbitratus*" ("I am sending you the theses of my friend, the theologian Martin Luther, which I believe deserve your authoritative judgment") (*Briefbuch*, 40). But in a letter to Kaspar Güttel, he is more explicit: "*paulatim quoque insinuo optimatum amicitiae d. M. Luder: eius conclusiones de indulgentiis admirantur ac in pretio habent Pirck-*

hamer, A. Tucher et Wenzeslaus, C. Nuzel traduxit, ego Augustam et Ingolstadium misi" ("Little by little I am also introducing Dr. Martin Luther to the friendship of the patricians; his theses on indulgences are favorably received, and Pirckheimer and Anton Tucher and Wenzeslaus have them for sale; C. Nützel has translated them; I have sent them to Augsburg and Ingolstadt") (*Briefbuch*, 43). It is completely out of the question that a recently released copy of the Ninety-five Theses, receipt of which is attested as of 5 January, should on 8 January already be admired among the "patricians" of the city, whose friendship Scheurl is *gradually* winning for Luther and that this copy could also be sent out in a new imprint.

g. It is not well established when Scheurl wrote the two letters to Luther for which Luther thanked him on 5 March 1518. Both of them are lost, the Latin as well as the German (*"binas ex te literas accepi . . . alteras latinas, alteras vernaculas"* ["I received two letters from you, one in Latin and the other in the vernacular"], Luther said [WABr 1:151]). Luther's letter of 11 December 1517 answers Scheurl's letter of 3 November (WABr 1:125), the last one of 1517. With one of these, Scheurl sent Luther the two imprints of the Ninety-five Theses in Latin and German. That the sending of them took place in January 1518 is to be assumed. The loss of the two letters is very regrettable. From them we should have more sure information about the Nuremberg imprints, as well as Scheurl's first acquaintance with the Ninety-five Theses. Luther's answer to Scheurl on 5 March and Scheurl's sending of the theses have a special point relative to the early history: Luther did not send Scheurl the Ninety-five Theses in their time, but despite that fact, Scheurl could present to Luther two Nuremberg imprints of them two-and-a-half months later. That explains Luther's relatively complete treatment of the matter.

From whom Scheurl had gotten the original copy of the *propositiones* to which the shipment of 5 November is indebted we do not know. In the letter to Eck he said merely that he had received them from Wittenberg. If it had been a direct transmission from Luther, with an added express direction to send them on to Eck, as in the case of the theses Against Scholastic Theology, we should expect a remark to that effect. The absence of such a remark again supports the assumption that this refers to the Ninety-five Theses. It is not surprising that Scheurl was in close touch with the University of Wittenberg; from 1507 to 1512 he had been not only professor and dean of the law faculty but also rector of the university. One of his Wittenberg acquaintances immediately shared the sensation with him, and Scheurl did his part to publicize it—apparently first in a written copy of 5 November, then at the beginning of January at once in two printed editions.

73 Here, too, to say it once more—really superfluously—only a plan for debate is mentioned and never any sort of ecclesiastical approval.

74 There are only three Latin reprints extant: in Leipzig, Nuremberg, and Basel; it must be assumed that the total number published must have been much larger. No imprint at all with a German translation of the theses is extant from that period.

75 The *Resolutions*.

76 At the end of March, Luther reported a visit of the abbot of Lehnin, who came as an emissary of the bishop of Brandenburg and asked him to delay somewhat the

publication of the *Resolutions* and all other writing on indulgences, not because they presumably contained something unorthodox but solely to avoid scandal. Luther said: "I was terribly embarrassed to have so great a bishop so humbly send so great an abbot to me. Only for this one reason did I say, 'I am satisfied; I would rather obey than perform miracles, even if I could, and do other things that might excuse my zeal.'" On his part the bishop was apparently so impressed by Luther's manner in this exchange that he did not oppose the publication much longer.

77 Apparently the "Sermon on Indulgence and Grace," which Luther must have written immediately after this letter, for it was already published when the abbot of Lehnin visited him.

To Jodocus Trutfetter, 9 May 1518

78 Joducus Trutfetter, Luther's teacher in Erfurt in 1507, then professor in Wittenberg; from there he returned very shortly to Erfurt; he was a representative of the nominalist branch of Scholasticism.

79 Lost.

80 "Sermon on Indulgence and Grace" (pp. 63f.).

81 Luther described the incident in his letter to Lang on 21 March 1518 (WABr 1:155): It concerned a student disturbance; a book dealer had tried to sell Tetzel's theses in Wittenberg and caused a student riot; they took away the eight hundred copies he had and burned them in the market.

To Pope Leo X, May 1518

82 Actually this is no real letter but one of the two introductions to the printed version of the *Resolutions* (the other, also in letter form, is addressed to Staupitz).

83 What Luther meant by this is not certain. According to his own words (p. 33 and in repeated parallel passages), he wrote only to bishops Albert and Jerome (the account of Myconius, whose value is still very much contested, is to the contrary, however). Still, the moment a person applies this sentence (and the following) to the chronology before the theses, that is, connects it with the incidents Luther speaks of in the first two sentences of his letter to the bishop of Brandenburg (p. 74), all the difficulties are eliminated. Indeed, these two utterances are considered real parallels.

84 Again, no word about sending the theses to the bishops is found; but debate is spoken of, as always.

85 A translation of the last section of the letter is given in *Reformation Writings of Martin Luther*, trans. Bertram Lee Woolf (London: Lutterworth, 1952), 1:65.

To Frederick the Wise, 21 (?) November 1518

86 The date is not very certain, but the differences involved amount to only a few days. More important than that is the fact that Luther wrote the letter at the request of Frederick the Wise and with the further purpose of sending it on to Cardinal Cajetan. It represents a procedure initiated by the court for the defense of

the elector against the cardinal. Only with this preliminary information can a person understand the letter correctly.

[87] Here we see how accurate Luther's anticipation was, about which he wrote to Spalatin in the preceding year (p. 71).

[88] This sentence is understood incorrectly if one interprets it with the emphasis on its last words. The emphasis lies on "not to the secular government." Luther was to prove that the elector had had nothing to do with the theses. If one wishes to take the sentence literally, the word *first* renders that impossible because there is no *second*. It was a tactical political utterance, and even at that not so much Luther's as the elector's, whose request Luther was answering. Also the rest of the letter proves that. Even the fact that Luther wrote to the elector in Latin—obviously he usually corresponded with him in German—proves that here he is speaking with windows open.

[89] Cf. the notes to the letter to Albert of Mainz, 31 October 1517 (pp. 110–14).

To Nicholas Amsdorf, 1 November 1527

[90] Luther was telling Amsdorf, who was in Magdeburg at the time, about the devastation of the plague in Wittenberg.

[91] For the sake of the importance attached to this excerpt for the hypothesis that the posting of the theses took place on 1 November 1517, we quote the full Latin text: "*Wittenbergae die Omnium Sanctorum, anno decimo Indulgentiarum conculcatarum, quarum memoria hac hora bibimus utrinque consolati.*" As the the matter turns out, the alleged content is not to be found. *Anno decimo* does not mean "ten years after" but "in the tenth year after." If Luther had intended to designate 1 November as the day of the posting, he would have expressed it differently according to all rules of grammar.

[92] All Saints' Day was still a festival (and for a long time after this); that easily explains the social gathering.

Luther's Words on the Theses in His Table Talk

[93] Next to the conclusion of the preceding letter (p. 80), two items from the Table Talk, nos. 2455a and 2455b, stand as the chief bases for the hypothesis of 1 November as the day of the posting of the theses. As long as they are handled as isolated passages, they might perhaps make some impression, though even then their meaning is immediately limited in view of the following consideration. The Feast of All Saints in the usage of that time (and in that of modern Roman Catholicism) begins on 31 October, that is, with the vigil, an essential part of the feast. Besides, the formula "I began to write against the pope and indulgences" can only be taken in a transferred sense. Luther must have begun with the writing of the theses long before the day of their posting, not just a little while beforehand.

If one considers the total applicable content of the Table Talk (as collected here for the first time), then the differences in evidence become very apparent. For the year 1516 as the terminus of "I began to write against the pope," we have the texts of nos. 884, 2250, 2255a, Part 2; other texts make general reference to 1517 (nos.

3644c, 5346, 6861); one particular text (no. 3722) speaks expressly of the day *after* All Saints. Other texts date the beginning of the entire conflict differently: no. 885 speaks of the year after the discussion with Staupitz about the doctorate (1513?); no. 2255a (Part 1 because Part 2 speaks of 1516); and 2255b speaks of a terminus two years after his doctorate (1514). One thing is clear: In part these sources are referring to different occurrences (in 1516, for instance, Luther preached a sermon against indulgences); but in part they do not distinguish dating precisely. In light of this fact, one cannot possibly build as much on one item of the Table Talk (no. 2455a; no. 2455b, the parallel passage, already speaks in generalities) as has been done in the modern discussion. The same source (the collection of Cordatus) has many other chronological approaches, and besides, no. 2255a is in conflict with itself.

Still the significance of the Table Talk should not be minimized. The collection almost always provides valuable information regarding the material we get from Luther's writings and letters, as well as other contemporary sources. That goes also for the statements of the Table Talk regarding the Ninety-five Theses and their early and later history. But it is also true that the Table Talk must be subjected to very careful scrutiny every time before its information can be used. Especially its parallel passages must be compared if a person wants to reconstruct the report that stands behind them (or, better yet, reports, for Luther referred to many events a number of times). It would take too long to deal in this manner with the full meaning of the reports given in this section. So far as the Ninety-five Theses are concerned, the texts in this volume, together with their introductions, provide the information necessary for such a reconstruction.

Preface to the 1538 Edition of the Theses

[94] After all the preceding material, this recollection of Luther from 1538 does not require a commentary except for the remark that two other editions (1530 and 1531) of the collected theses of Luther had preceded the 1538 edition. Those had not been produced at Luther's instigation and were introduced by a preface of Melanchthon. The collection of 1538, too, was only tolerated by Luther. He added a preface to it only because he wanted the theses of an earlier day to be put in the right light. His manner reminds us of his preface of 1545 (p. 31), yet we receive valuable information and impressions above and beyond that document. After the detailed information of the letters and Table Talk, this preface once again sets before our eyes the whole context to which Luther's Ninety-five Theses belong.

Exhortation to the Clergy Assembled at the Imperial Diet of Augsburg, 1530

[95] Luther composed this work in the first two weeks of his residence at the Coburg as a reminder to the participants at the Imperial Diet at Augsburg, to which he himself could not go because he was under the ban. As the first installment, eight hundred copies came to Augsburg from Wittenberg and were sold immediately. Prohibition of the promulgation of the work achieved nothing; at once it was in the hands "of all pious men with the approval of God and men, to the distress of Satan

gnashing his teeth," as Justus Jonas reported to Luther from Augsburg, 13 June 1530. Luther's manuscript is still extant, which we follow (though most of the spelling differences between it and the first edition are insignificant to us). Here Luther once more looked back to the beginning, to the situation before his attack on indulgences, as well as the progressive changes occasioned by it in the life of the church and of each individual believer. Here we no doubt go beyond the bounds of the stated theme of this book. Yet our theme and the whole book thus really achieve the right emphasis. For the Ninety-five Theses are rightly understood only if we see them in connection with the changes they wrought.